Curious Men
Lost in the Congo

Also by
Bob Kunzinger

The Iron Scar: A Father and Son in Siberia
A Third Place: Notes in Nature
Blessed Twilight: Vincent Van Gogh
Penance
Borderline Crazy: Essays

CURIOUS MEN
LOST IN THE CONGO

Bob Kunzinger

Lake Dallas, Texas

Copyright © 2026 by Bob Kunzinger
All rights reserved
Printed in the United States of America

FIRST EDITION

Author's Note:

This is a true story as I remember and recorded the events. The Belgian Congo gained independence in 1960. From 1971 to 1997 the country was officially the Republic of Zaire, a change made by then ruler Gen. Mobutu Sese Seko. In 1997, the name was changed again to what it is known as today, The Democratic Republic of the Congo. Since the events within this text occurred in the early 1980's, I use the name Zaire.

Requests for permission to reprint or reuse material
from this work should be sent to:

Permissions
Madville Publishing
PO Box 358
Lake Dallas, TX 75065

Cover Design: Jacqueline Davis

ISBN: 978-1-963695-43-4 paperback,
978-1-963695-44-1 ebook

Library of Congress Control Number: 2025945664

For Joe:

*No man ever steps in the same river twice,
for it's not the same river and he's not the same man.*

—Heraclitus

*How is it possible to bring order
out of memory?*

—Beryl Markham

Table of Contents

1	Prologue
9	Arrival
28	Antonio's
42	Fly
50	Education
60	Language
69	Alone
75	Mountains of the Moon
82	The Explorers
92	Once
94	Departure
97	Letters
105	Nineteen
112	Lost in the Present Tense
117	Acclimation
126	Transition
127	In Country
132	How to Die in the Congo
140	The Congo River
152	Epilogue—It's been a journey.
159	About the Author

Prologue

I have no idea how to tell this story correctly. Joe was an animated person, so full of life that my instinct has always been to first capture that part of his character so the reader would understand the energy that radiated from us both when I was a freshman in college. I need to illuminate the magnetic personality of Joseph Kohn, how he absorbed attention everywhere he went. At the same time, I want to demonstrate my own ghost-like existence at nineteen years-old, my trepidation in doing the smallest of activities outside of my comfort zone, and my isolation four hundred miles from home.

Instead, I chose to start with how it should have ended had everything gone the way we planned, which, of course, rarely happens—particularly when you're nineteen and twenty-seven years old. The flow of this work delves deeply into the pure state of being alive I experienced while planning this great adventure on the Congo River, the excitement, the laughter, the absolute conviction that our destiny was our own to decide. Only this way am I able to focus on the exceptional period of brilliant possibilities that played out that year back when we were too young to know better.

It was supposed to end like this:

It the Fall of 1981, my junior year in college was about to start. That semester was a long one, not just for the exams and papers, but for the waiting. The previous fall, Joe Kohn and I had sat in a stairwell, silent, waiting for the taxi to take him to the airport for a flight to Africa for his solo journey on the Congo River in Zaire. After he left, I had contacted the press in Buffalo, New York, and Washington, D.C. I called Voice of America, *National Geographic*, and *Geo*. Finally, in January, a letter arrived from Joe. He had written it while in Kolwezi, which he should have passed much earlier, but I didn't worry about that; we knew the weather conditions could cause delay, and we were hyperaware of the areas threatened by remnants of war. Honestly, we knew almost everything we needed to assure his success, including the possibility of changes to the schedule. So, in the January letter I wasn't surprised by Joe's enthusiasm to finish. He emphasized that he had only another month or so of hard paddling before it was smooth sailing all the way to Kinshasa and on to Banana Beach on the Atlantic.

The next several months of waiting were oppressive, until finally in early April, a call came through to my dorm. The Peace Corps director in Kinshasa told me Joe had just left the city and started his final leg toward the coast. I was to fly to Kinshasa on May 5th.

The anticipation muddled my attempts to study for finals, but I finished and rode a Bluebird Bus from the Olean station to Kennedy Airport where I made notes and read stories from newspapers about Joe, the first person to ever canoe the entire Congo River alone. Most of the trip had gone as planned, but some unexpected waterfalls north of Lumbumbashi had slowed him down, and just past Kolwezi he had gotten lost for several weeks. It turned out he was headed toward Angola. When he went over the falls early on, his compass got ruined, so he relied upon the sun for direction, but even that was not reliable. Some villagers south of Bukavu gave him food and rest before setting him straight. The river traffic heading toward Kinshasa was predictably dangerous. Twice he had been swamped, but by then he had learned his lesson and kept his goods sealed in plastic bags a friend in Bukavu had given him. When he met his Kinshasa contacts, he left them his journals, his film, and anything else he didn't need, and asked them to call me. And a week after I arrived in Kinshasa, Joe met me in a café. The area was busier than I had anticipated. It was not so hot yet, but the sun was strong, and the traffic left us all hotter. I almost didn't recognize him. But then Joe stood close, raised high a bottle of water, his smile stretching like the Congo River itself from one end to the other, and I could breathe again. I smiled at what was left of my emaciated, tired friend, and we embraced. A crowd of travelers had already gathered, eating fish and drinking—all completely engrossed in Joe's story. The café became more intimate, and the conversation continued long into the night. People took pictures they promised to send. Two reporters spent most of the evening talking to us, but at the end of the night just Joe and I sat in the peace of the beachfront town. I had phone calls to make. He needed to call his parents. We sat in the café and listened to the quiet motion of the African night. Later, near dawn, we walked along the square toward the hotel for breakfast, and Joe broke the silence.

"Did you get the maps of the Amazon?" he asked. We laughed, and then he turned to me, smiling, and said, "We did it."

Pure fiction. I made all of that up; it never happened. Still, it is curious how close imagination and memory can be, like best friends with conflicting points of view.

In those first few years after I returned from Kolwezi, Zaire, especially when I was tired, Joe's story ended like this:

March of '81 came and went. Then April. Then summer. I returned to college for the fall semester and called Joe's parents. They still had not heard anything and were getting ready to call the State Department. I decided to phone Washington myself, and after circulating through the maze of operators, they told me no information could be given to non-family members.

A few weeks later I called Joe's parents again.

Joe had died.

His parents told me that he had arrived in Kolwezi tired, fighting a case of worms, his boat in horrible shape, patched together with inner tubes. After just a few days, he pushed back into the river to continue his journey, but a worried Peace Corps volunteer asked a Zairean friend to follow him for a while. The river winds and bends, and not far after Kolwezi it branches like veins draining into the vastness of Africa. A week later, the man returned to the village saying Joe had fallen very ill, was vomiting, and could no longer move very well. He wouldn't even eat anymore. By the time anyone got out to him the next day, he was not there.

He was never found.

I took out the maps and circled the area with a pen. He did not get very far. Not far at all.

This isn't so much fiction as it is fictionalized. Yet, this version is probably closer to the truth, though the distance between what I know and what I will never be able to know can never be fully breached. It leaves me awake sometimes contemplating, considering, but never with clarity or certainty, even these forty plus years later. Knowing almost everything is often more damaging than knowing nothing at all.

In three separate but identical dreams over the course of six months or so, it ended like this:

I sat in the car of a Peace Corps volunteer reading Joe's letter again, listening to his voice in my mind. "Bob, this is BIG! BIG! BIG!" it reads. I sat quietly a few minutes. I was in Kolwezi. Across the street was a small tree-filled park, with benches, and some women set up stands to sell linen, fruit, bread and other goods. The rain had stopped, and it was warm.

I walked around a few streets, at first foolishly looking for Joe, then realizing where I was. A few weeks earlier I was in West Africa, no intention on heading this far south. Now, I walked streets in southern Zaire wondering what to do next. I could smell fruit, and nearby a woman sold mangos. I walked through the park along a dirt path lined with trees. Green benches interrupted the patches of grass and dirt, and a woman asked me to buy some fruit. I kept walking. Just past her about three benches on the left someone sat in a brown leather coat despite the heat, and I sat down next to him.

It was Joe.

He turned and smiled, but half his face was gone; the left half completely gone right to the cheek bone. His good eye, the right one, opened wider when he recognized me. I said, "I have been looking for you." He was thin, sickly thin, and his hair was very short, cut nearly to the scalp.

He leaned closer and whispered, "Bob, *I* have been looking for *you*."

This one woke me up every time. You see, I can recall the vibrant energy we had at the start while planning the journey, so I am haunted by the contrast. We swam the Allegheny pretending it was the Congo; we ate sundried fish; we spoke Lingala; we memorized diseases; we kept silent for days on end; we laughed for days on end. Everyone knew who we were and what we were doing, and the support was unwavering. I went from an isolated, terrified nineteen year-old four hundred miles from home to a player in the heart of a world-class adventure, and it was an unbreakable time back then. So, this one wakes me up and tugs at my facts, teasing them into a more disheveled and disastrous shape.

So here is truth:

The last letter I received from Joe was in January 1981. The State Department started a search later that summer, and continued sporadically looking for Joe in Zaire, surrounding countries, and even in the United States for the next two years. The Red Cross had been contacted, as had all Peace Corps sites, local governments, and police. All searches turned up negative.

Later, I traveled to Africa and met some people with whom I had mutual friends. We sat around a table one night, drinking Flagg Beer and talking about the dilapidated African infrastructure. It mattered. Once again, they asked of my interest in Africa, and once again I told the story. I started with Joe's bike trip from Buffalo to South America, and about a night Joe and I spent in an Italian restaurant drawing maps on the backs of place mats. I spoke of his three years living in Zaire, mastering the languages, the culture, the nuances of give and take in the remote, dangerous territory not long before the Shaba Province uprisings. I told of the year he and I spent in western New York preparing in every way possible for his trip; how we anticipated the best and prepared for the worst—so well that I could have taken the trip myself. They told me all about their experiences in Zaire, who to talk to, who to avoid. They told me who they knew that was heading that way, and why, and how traveling with someone who knew the languages made more sense.

Sometime later, I stood waist deep in the Congo River, staring west over rocks and probably bones. I was frightened and wished to be anywhere else: back around that table, at the airport, or in western New York eating and drinking at a small Italian restaurant, drawing on placemats and swimming in the Allegheny River.

Young boys threw nets while women washed clothes. The dirty, warm water ran past my thighs, and I spotted a man washing shirts over the edge of a canoe. It is pointless, I thought, and I waded to shore and walked into a nearby park where trees and benches lined dirt paths and women sold fruit.

I turned and stared back at the river awhile. Young men and women walked by carrying bags, laughing. It brought to mind our planning and excitement when a current of certainty flowed strong through us; this all should have played out differently. I continued on the path and sat on a bench just past a woman selling mangos.

Whenever I tell this story, which isn't often anymore, someone always asks if I ever found him. I simply move on to something else, sometimes including the story about trying to sell eight-foot-long tusks in a mall, other times I leave that one out and include the one about stopping by a friend's farm at three in the morning and four of us hanging out drinking wine and drawing each other's feet. That was right before he left, right before we never saw him again. Ever since an excerpt appeared in the *Alabama Literary Review*, sometimes someone will thank me for understanding their lack of closure, their inability to know the concrete reality of death. A child of theirs is missing, they will tell me, or, on one occasion, a brother is still MIA in Vietnam. All I can do is nod and listen. They understand the thin line between a happy reunion and never coming home again.

So, I tell it again—each time starting in a different place—like Joe's bike ride to South America, or our near drowning incident in Lake Chautaqua, and then I'll add another story. Like the time we sat on my floor with hundreds of malachite hearts and raw rubies and dozens of yellow and smoked topaz stones spread around, and we laughed trying to figure out what they'd sell for; or the time we drove to a concert in Buffalo and a reporter took him aside to ask about "this crazy trip I've heard about."

Not too long ago, a writer I respect suggested that the narrative must end at the river. "It's what keeps the story flowing through your life," he said. "And Joe's!" He told me, "Bob, the river is the antagonist, Joe the protagonist, and you, my friend, are the only dynamic character in the story."

But it's not a story to me, it's memory. And while I tell what happened, the narrative is incomplete. There is no ending—no falling action, no resolution. Besides, my friend had one detail wrong: no matter how I remember or don't remember the events of the day-to-day planning in western New York or later on my own trip to the Congo on a seemingly pointless quest, it doesn't *end* at the river; the river is where it *starts*.

One

Arrival

For thirty-five years I've been staring at nineteen-year-old college students, and I never miss the chance to provide them with examples of how old I am. For instance, when my family moved from Long Island eight hours south to Virginia Beach, my old friends in New York were simply gone; out of my life. If I didn't write a physical letter and mail it at the post office, or if I couldn't convince my parents to let me pick up the phone and call long distance, I never heard from them again. That's just the way it was. I moved on and, seemingly, grew up a little, forced to find my own way forward without them. As a result I learned to make new friends, explore different paths and find my footing without the security of people I've known since birth. At this point in the story, my class usually appears dumbfounded that I'd actually "lose touch" with someone. I let them know that it was normal back when all that connected you to others was a rotary phone, and moving away meant severing ties with the kids on the block. During that first summer in the south three months before school started, I tell them, I didn't know a soul, and at fifteen-years-old could not drive. It was me, my bike, and the beach.

But by the time that mid-July rolled around, I clocked

sixty and seventy miles a day on my ten-speed Huffy, mostly either along the boardwalk, through a state park, or to the tennis courts at a nearby high school so I could practice my serves to an empty receiving court. That summer was all about being alone and seeking adventures on my own, not by choice but by my ability to fit it to the neighborhood clique and my disinterest in sitting around. I canoed the river behind our house, I wandered the beach, and I escaped on the bike, riding further each day. At some point I learned of a new cross-country bike trail known then as the Bikecentennial Trail from Williamsburg, Virginia, to the coast of Oregon. I found something to believe in, even if I knew my parents would never let it happen.

Later that summer, a college friend of my sister's came to visit from western New York. His Dutch-cut, dirty blond hair and small round glasses made him look like John Denver, and since my sister was still working for a few days, Joe and I spent time together during the day cruising on our bikes around Virginia Beach or up to the tennis courts at a nearby high school. In fact, he made the trip from his farm in North Collins, New York, to Virginia, on his bike.

He told me about that ride, and then he told me about his ride to South America, about ten-thousand miles in all, from Buffalo to Brazil, and he talked always with his infectious smile and a quiet enthusiasm for everything. I had no stories; I had two passions at sixteen years old: tennis and biking. I told him I wanted to ride across the country to Coos Bay, Oregon, on the new trail created to commemorate the two hundredth anniversary of the signing of the Declaration of Independence. I had maps, and he insisted we get them out and study them together. He told me how to handle the traffic, the mountains, the wind. He said that I seemed to be in shape and probably wouldn't have too much trouble since east to west, while into the prevailing breezes, allowed time to acclimate to the climbs, reaching the not-so-high Appalachians, then the plains, and only then the Rockies. Joe was the first person to take me seriously. He laughed and told me it was exactly what I should do without ever addressing my age or the ridicule I might endure from others. He spoke as if *of course* I would go if that were my plan, as if all American young men should ride a bike thousands of miles. At a time I found myself detached from everything I had ever known, someone came along who had been around the block, and he was the first person to take my dreams seriously, not humoring me by agreeing with whatever I suggested, but talking me through the steps. Joe was sure of himself. He helped me to be surer of myself. It works like that. And he came along just as I was floundering, knew no one, and for the first time in my life, found myself pretty much alone nearly all the time.

We lay on the living room floor one day with my map of the United States with markings from Virginia to the Pacific, and he nodded as if he were taking the trip himself. "I need your help," I told him. I didn't realize it at the time, but what I needed was his confidence, that internal motivation which kept spilling out of him.

He told me his post-graduate plans for that following year were to join the Peace Corps. He wanted to go to Africa. I don't remember knowing what the Peace Corps was at the time. My few interests beyond bikes and tennis courts included music and journalism. In high school, we read Woodward and Bernstein's *All the President's Men* and Jack Reed's *Ten Days that Shook the World*, so my ambitions were to be an investigative journalist; to travel the world, starting with Coos Bay, Oregon, and write about it, unearth truths everyone would need to know. St.

Bonaventure University, which Joe and my sister attended, had an excellent journalism program, so I decided I'd go there. I'd been there once in the summer of 1972 when my family dropped my sister off at the college for the first time. I can clearly recall sitting on a chair outside the room at the Castle Motel across from campus in the chilly August evening air and falling in love with those "Enchanted Mountains." So when Joe spoke of college and the river and the hills behind campus, and when he talked about his family farm not far from there, I could visualize it, felt as if I already knew the area seeing as how other than Long Island and Virginia, it was the only place I had ever been. We looked at my maps and I was paying attention to everything he said.

I met Joe very briefly one more time the following May at my sister's graduation from St. Bonaventure before he left for Africa with the Peace Corps. Several years passed and we lost touch as was the way then. I remembered him from time to time as I delayed and then abandoned the bike ride. I learned to drive, and after high school I decided to delay college as well, mostly out of boredom, for what today we call a "gap year." It's a long ride from fifteen to eighteen years old, so that by the time I ended up in the journalism department at St. Bonaventure at nineteen, Joe had become little more than someone I used to know, briefly, through someone else. I didn't even know his family hadn't heard from in quite some time as he meandered from Africa to South America; nor would I have cared that much. It was normal back then to be out of touch; people weren't attached with a wireless umbilical. Being "out of touch" today is measured in hours or minutes. When I was nineteen it could be weeks, sometimes months or years, and depending on the circumstance and the person, no one worried. Some friends were gone completely, and you didn't really concern yourself with it; maybe you'd run into each other again one day, but doubtful.

Four years after that summer I spent in the south, I moved to western New York to start my freshman year in college. I thought I was the only one who felt terrified. Now that I've been staring at nineteen-year-olds for thirty-five years as a college professor, I have stood witness to some common traits among the campus newbies. First and foremost, they're *all* terrified, even the confident ones—often especially the confident ones. The problem is they don't know what to do about it or what questions to ask. And even if they did, they have no comfort in numbers yet, still faking it on their own, so they adjust to this virgin lifestyle by acting older and more knowledgeable than they should, or, more commonly today, regressing online to childish antics with childhood friends easily found in the palm of their hands, their phone their security blanket and a lifeline to reassuring friends who consistently respond with "You got this." No, they don't. Add to their raw introduction to adult life the notion that a convoy of adults they never met before simultaneously pounds them with new expectations, from living on their own for the first time, to eating healthy, sleeping well, not partying too much, studying, going to classes, figuring out their major, applying for internships and scholarships and part-time jobs, then add to that the required course assignments, exams, and meeting an entirely new mob of people, a good deal of whom they're going to live with, share a bathroom with, get homesick in front of, and get sick with all within a few weeks, it's quite common to feel a tad overwhelmed.

Welcome to college. Strap yourself in.

It wasn't too much different in the fall of 1979 when my parents drove me from the beaches of southeastern Virginia to the small village of Allegany, New York. And for the second time in four years I once again cut all ties with everyone I knew four hundred miles from home. My friends with whom I came of age, had crushes on, confided in, were all suddenly gone, fifteen years before cellphones. Today, when students get nervous they can contact a friend from home. Back then if we got nervous, we had no such connections to lean on.

Most of my classmates at the college were from just a few hours away; Buffalo, Rochester, Syracuse. No one save me was from south of the Mason Dixon Line. So my floormates either knew one another or at the very least were from the same town, knew the same people and hangouts, rooted for the same teams. I immediately felt like an outsider, and my friends back home simply did not exist from August until December.

One more thing: The drinking age was eighteen.

At college, I didn't like my dorm at first and I had trouble getting to know most of my floormates, whose attention that first year was mostly focused on getting drunk and destroying property. I avoided the dark side of college life by making friends with priests or faculty and hiking the hills around campus. In classes I was bored nearly immediately. I saw absolutely no practical application to anything in class, such as how to write a process essay; English class bored me while I simmered in the back of my science class truly not caring about the different types of rocks, and except for the few journalism courses on my schedule, I simply didn't bother doing the necessary work, or I would merely slip by with just what I had to. My first semester ended with a note of probation to get my grades up. Worse, the college sent my parents a bill for the damage done to the floor—broken windows, doors, destroyed toilets and urinals, more, from four months of keg parties. The total bill was split evenly amongst everyone's parents, but the Dean of Students was kind enough to send a separate letter to my folks which explained that while the bill was necessary, I had nothing to do with any of it. My floormates learned about those "exception letters" a few of our parents received, and it segregated some of us even further.

The whole college thing simply wasn't working out. I had fun to be sure: I got involved playing my guitar, I worked at the radio station, spent time with new friends in other, less toxic dorms. But at nineteen years old I felt pressure from absolutely everywhere to already know what I wanted to do with my life, what my path would be to get there, and how I was anticipating the following three years, graduate plans, career plans. I could not wrap my mind around this need for us to completely balance the world on our heads literally months after leaving high school where we finished our first eighteen years of life with almost no responsibilities. No wonder so many freshmen crash and burn. They're expected to smoothly absorb changes in every aspect of life with little or no rules or guidance. Colleges and family support centers might suggest there are plenty of resources available to help, but most teenagers who are finally on their own are not going to admit they need assistance. And even if they know they need help, they're not sure exactly why. So I escaped when I could, comfortable in the role of loner. I found myself thinking again about my bike ride west.

I went through the motions, attempted to suppress my attention difficulties every teacher since kindergarten told my parents about. It was always, "Robert pays too much attention to those around him in class." That never stopped, and if universities could send notes home to parents, mine would have still said the same thing. But I was a college student now, and I decided to suck it up and get through with my head down, as focused as possible. More than a few times I almost dropped out, decided I'd tell my parents I was biking to Oregon. But the arts saved me: I played coffeehouses, I DJ'd at the radio station, and I wrote for the newspaper. This all helped me tolerate my miserable living conditions and absolute boredom in the classroom.

My first year first semester classes included English Comp, Intro to Journalism, Sociology 101, Art History, and Philosophy. I liked my professors; I took all early morning classes, so I'd be done and out hiking before my floormates had even gotten out of bed for their afternoon classes. I showered in a bathroom I shared with fifty or sixty other guys where the windows had been busted out; in the winter it got cold. The one phone on the floor for nearly one hundred of us was a payphone at the junction in the hallway, and if anyone bothered to answer it when it rang, there was no guarantee the receiver worked or wasn't covered in shaving cream. On Friday nights it wasn't unusual for a half dozen of the non-drinking guys to be "pennied" into their rooms. That is when someone pushes the door to the room tight and shoves pennies between the door and the door jam, making it impossible to open the door from inside. The victim—sometimes me—would have to bang on the door until someone answered it, someone alone in the hallway or willing to suffer the ridicule of others watching and hoping the trapped one would never, ever get out. To make matters worse, the rooms had no toilets. I remember once someone had been pennied into his room and no one was around for hours on end until he finally opened his window and threw a chair out into the courtyard when he saw a priest walking by. The startled good father figured out the issue pretty quickly and answered his plea.

This was college life. This was prime time. This is what my floormates lived for. I wasn't interested.

During orientation—a cross between valuable information during the day and hazing at night—the first Friday at the end of the first full week of classes, the doors to our floor on our wing of the dorm were locked, and all the new students were told to stand on a crate at the junction of the hall and drink until they threw up. When my turn came, I stood on the crate, took a sip of beer, and stepped down. I was pushed back up and held by my arms. I told them I didn't drink, and after a small battle, returned to my room. My roommate returned after he drank four or five glasses and everyone applauded, and said, "You're not very popular here, you know." Steve and I got along very well, and he said that as an observation, not a criticism.

"Yeah, no kidding," I said.

"You don't drink?"

"Only when *I* decide to."

"They're good guys, you know. They're just messing around."

"Maybe. But it's a control thing. I guess I don't want to give that up. Maybe I saw *Cool Hand Luke* too many times," I said, and we laughed.

He smiled, then he laughed to himself; a laugh of approval it seemed. "Come on," he said. "Let's go to the skellar and I'll buy you a beer." And we did.

I'd seen *Animal House*, so this wasn't unexpected. But I ran into something it took me a very long time to understand: my floormates were good people. Smart. Kind. Even humble; the old shirt-off-their-back kind of guys. They worked hard at their studies, and many of them went on to become highly successful and deeply caring and giving people. But at nineteen, we simply had different definitions of adventure, of excitement. I had a strong conviction that no adventure should come at the expense of anyone else through ridicule or embarrassment, and I was easily embarrassed back then and often scared I was always doing something the wrong way. I just didn't have the vocabulary to express that at the time any more than freshman in college can today. Instead, I simply felt out of place, and I didn't have the maturity to put together the concepts to understand what was wrong. Mostly, the others left me alone because I played music and worked at the radio station; activities they communally agreed were "acceptable" for one of their floormates. But I wanted to ride out of there and never return. I saw no point to it all, any of it. I wasn't suicidal, but I did want that part of my life to die; I just didn't yet know what I should do instead. Floundering again.

For thirty-five years I've been staring at nineteen-year-olds who more often than not see me first among all of their college professors. So what I say to them, how they perceive that first day their first semester their first time away from home, can carry some weight.

My first class at college was Introduction to Journalism. The professor, Dr. Russell Jandoli, started the program at the college decades earlier, had been an editor at *Stars and Stripes* during World War Two, and taught with a quiet control of a man who knew the answers to any question you could possibly throw at him without needing to let you know he was that good. He was the real thing.

The first day of classes he called roll, paused, and said, "There is no such thing as objectivity. It doesn't exist." Then he put on his small, black hat, picked up his books, and left. We waited a few minutes until one of the students saw him walking up the sidewalk toward the parking lot. "He's gone," he said. We sat a few more minutes, then we left.

Maybe this won't be so bad, I thought.

St. Bonaventure University sits in the foothills of the Allegheny Mountains of the Southern Tier of New York State. The rolling green hills and usual deep blue skies sit in contrast to the hazy, hot, and humid beaches of southeastern Virginia I had been used to. Old Route 17 meandered across the bottom of the state, moving west through Elmira then another one hundred miles to Olean, the college's large neighbor, and then through Allegany, the village most associated with St. Bonaventure. Another hour west is Jamestown. An hour or so north is Buffalo. Bradford, Pennsylvania, is just under an hour to the southwest. Simply put, the college is an hour from anything. At that time, cable television was brand new and not readily available on campus, personal computers were more than a decade away. So, activities included skiing at the nearest slope, sledding in the hilly university graveyard, hanging out in each other's rooms, playing sports in the facility, and drinking—St. Bonaventure's favorite pastime back then, either at the dangerously hot and crowded rathskeller beneath the dining hall on campus, or at one of the half dozen taverns in town. At roughly two in the morning then, when everything closed, the campus briefly became loud with drunk students lacking inhibitions and come morning one might find several floormates passed out in the hallway, the stairwell, or even in the open quad in the middle of the dorm. Weather is irrelevant when you're drunk.

Luckily, the ministry center on campus remained open

twenty-four hours a day; a convenience for those of us who slept on one of its couches when floor parties continued until dawn or when someone pulled one of the bi-weekly fire alarms sending everyone else out into a few feet of snow on wintry nights. The ministry was a welcome room of respite, as were the hills behind campus, including what everyone called "Merton's Heart." The great spiritual writer and monk, Thomas Merton, had taught at the college briefly before being called to his vocation. He would hike to the clearing and write in his journal. It is a quiet spot even today to sit and look down upon campus, despite the reality that sometimes on clear nights in the late '70s, the music of The Ramones, The Stray Cats, and The Clash, poured out the windows, past the ballfields, and across the river.

The Allegheny River.

Between campus and the hills sat the artery that not only ran past campus, but through my life for four years. It was my escape, my reminder that at the very worst, I could just get a raft and float away. Most of my pictures from my college days are of tree branches leaning hard over the rippling waters behind campus.

The headwaters are in north central Pennsylvania and the river runs north, through Elmira, then Bell Curves southwest about 325 miles towards Pittsburgh. The name comes from the Lenape and means both "Best flowing river of the hills" and "Beautiful River." Historically, it is considered the headwaters of the Ohio River, and the Iroquois considered the two the same river. In fact, in the Seneca language, which is the primary influence on the Southern Tier, the Allegheny River is pronounced "O-hi-o."

Behind the campus and through the village of Allegany back in 1979, this narrow and shallow river was lined with trees and mounds so that it was difficult to get too close to the edge of the water for most of the walk, but even today when you can get to the water, it is possible to wade across even when the river is running strong. The rocky bottom makes for an uneasy traverse, and it widens further downstream, eventually merging with the Ohio River near Pittsburgh.

In 1972, when my family brought my sister to the college her first year, Hurricane Agnes had flooded the river the previous June. The entire campus had been covered in river water, the floor of the basketball arena destroyed, and the banks of the Allegheny redefined. It turns out that even on a small waterway in the hills of New York, it doesn't take much for a river to disrupt lives after even just a few days of rain.

At some places trees bent freely over the banks, reaching out to meet their counterparts stretching from the southern bank along River Road. I spent a good deal of my college years either in or on the river, or on its crusty banks playing guitar, sometimes reading, sometimes just sitting peacefully, safely imagining other places.

The library stood as another option to escape the lunacy of long, alarming nights. It was nearly always open and remained busy for similar reasons. I never had the patience to study there, but I visited often, wandering to the basement to meander through the archives. In those lower hallways was the Franciscan Institute, which includes volumes of original writings dating back to the twelfth century. Also downstairs in the archives when I first arrived at campus was Fr. Irenaeus Herscher, librarian, and the keeper of institutional memory. Whenever I had a question for Dr. Jandoli or one of the other journalism profs, they'd send me to Fr. Irenaeus. He had been a friend of Thomas Merton's and was a quiet and consistent voice of reason. He died my sophomore year, but the atmosphere in those stacks beneath the library was one I sought often.

The other escape from dormitory rowdiness and vomit turned out to be the most endearing one for me. One night I walked through the long trail in the woods to the east of the main campus to Franics Hall. Once a seminary, it became a dorm with its own chapel and cafeteria only a few years earlier. The trail out there in 1979 was narrow and dark and it was more common to see skunks than students. At Francis, the basement, second, third, and fourth floors were living areas, but the first floor had the dining room, the chapel, a few offices, an art classroom, and the resident director's apartment. Beneath the chapel and under the art classroom was a former library for the seminarians which art instructor James Cole Young turned into his studio. Today, the late artist's work hangs throughout the world, but at the time he was just a late-twenty something, long haired, pot-smoking painter who loved to talk and loved an audience. We became close friends, and instead of weekend nights trying not to drink, I spent them playing guitars with Cole until three in the morning, watching him paint, listening to him rant about world politics, only to turn soft on a dime when a song came on which touched his soul.

Everyone found their place on campus, and often they overlapped. At basketball games, coffeehouses, in the Hickey Dining Hall, you'd see floormates who perhaps twelve hours earlier harassed you right in your own "home," where both of you lived, yet out in public they might nod hello, ask how the food is that day. I am not sure why no one else seemed to have a problem with this contrast, but I was simply not comfortable in this new world where drinking until you're sick and passing out in the hallway was as high as most of my floormates seemingly set the bar. I had no clue back then that drinking heavily was their version of hiking to the clearing behind campus to escape the pressure and insecurity.

I was not homesick. I had no desire to head back to Virginia Beach. I was floundering, disappointed that everything I hoped college would be could not be found anywhere, but I loved being on my own. Eventually, for the first time since moving from Long Island to Virginia Beach, I turned to my bicycle. I rode into Olean and played tennis at the racquet club much like I had done at fifteen when I rode to the high school to practice my serves. I rode through town to the other side of the river and up the four-lane to Cole's farm where I'd find him painting in the barn, or his wife Sharon picking apples on the hills behind their home. I rode sometimes well past Olean and out into the eastern countryside, and a few times I rode to Allegheny State Park to rent a cabin for the weekend. I had good friends, to be sure, some of which are still close. But back then, back there, I was absolutely lost. Something was missing.

The next meeting of Dr. Jandoli's Intro to Journalism course found all of us completely at attention. He called roll, then asked, "Miss Philipps, what is there no such thing as?"

Sally answered. "Objectivity."

"And how do you know that, Miss Philipps."

"You told us on Monday." We all laughed. So did he.

"You just made my point."

Years later I told him about that lesson and how I never forgot it. He said we were going to become journalists and there was no more important information for us to know than we are not being objective even when we try to be. He didn't want that information lost amidst the other information we had no intention of retaining. I was intrigued. He explained how our view of the world is defined from early on by our family's economic status, numbers of siblings and if we were the oldest or the youngest, if we lived in the country or the city, everything. He had my attention.

23

Still, the course turned boring fast. I just wanted to write, or at the very least learn about writing. I wasn't interested in theory or the history of journalism back to the Roman days. I understood the differences between the role of a university as opposed to a certificate program, but those same identifiers which helped our university degree stand apart from one year or even two-year college programs happen to be the same courses which put me to sleep. Astronomy. Christian Marriage. Media Law. Epistemology and Metaphysics.

In the other classes it was the same, so that I did what I had to in order to pass, then took off on my bike for the hills, or headed to Niagara and Lockport in a borrowed car. One friend had a blue VW Beetle, so one weekend to avoid the parties we drove to nearby Alfred University where one of my cousins was a senior, found him, and ended up drinking in *their* rathskeller. It was different, though. The focus was family. Back at my college, alcohol was the focus. Ironically, I did poorly in classes that first semester and all of my drunken stupor floormates had high grades. Go figure.

Cleary it was me; the problem was me. I know this now.

Just as we were headed home for winter break to spend Christmas with our families and see high school friends for the first time in four months, catching up in someone's garage or at the boardwalk, it occurred to me that it wasn't the students drinking and partying all night that was out of place; I was. They were just blowing off steam from the pressure they probably faced trying to make the grade. No one had ever put pressure on me; and while I didn't do well that semester, I didn't do well because I simply didn't bother, not because I couldn't. Most of my floormates had no options except to succeed. Maybe I was simply one helicopter parent away from alcoholism.

Nothing—I mean nothing at all—challenged me. While I criticized my floormates for setting their bar so low that you only had to drink until you got sick to surpass it, it was still higher than my own ambitions, which at that point in my life were as vague as the hills behind campus on a misty morning. It occurred to me that the rampant drinking on my floor and even in town was the result of their bar being set for them by their parents, and always attempting to please others required a definitive and proven escape, like drinking. Still, I was lost, and I felt at the time like I couldn't do a damn thing about it but go home for the holidays and return three weeks later and suffer it all again.

That winter break freshman year was illuminating for one crystal clear reality—I much preferred the haphazard chaos of dorm life to being home with my parents again. They were fine, and I loved them and we all got along well, but it took one trip home after four months away for the first time in my life to appreciate floormates who didn't give a rat's ass what I did, friends who enjoyed sitting around in a room doing nothing, and the freedom to wander at will in western New York, even Canada, or hang out until dawn in the studio of a stoned artist. No kidding, I missed my drunk floormates. I couldn't wait to get back, no matter how monotonous and uninteresting it was. I hoped the good stuff in classes would come and we would dive deep into the writing process, albeit in another year or so. But my attention was on using college resources to play coffeehouses and borrowing friend's cars to head to Niagara; both became my version of getting drunk.

One Friday morning, the first week in February, I fell asleep in Dr. Shepard's sociology class, which was ironic since it was the one class I enjoyed. He caught my attention early on when he said he was running a study tour to the Yucatan Peninsula. I had called my father, and he said I could go. In the end the trip never had enough students for it to materialize, but for a little while anyway it gave me a reason to show up to the one class which suddenly had relevance to my immediate future. But that morning, the newness and excitement of being back on my own in college had quickly worn off, and I stared out the window toward blankness, and I listened to a barrage of nothingness as I dozed in and out. If he called on me for anything I didn't know about it.

Class ended and he woke me up. I shook my head to the reality that it was just him and me in the room, and he laughed. "Out drinking too much, Bob?" he asked.

"Umm. No. Um, no sir. No, I don't drink that much. I tried to sleep in the ministry because of the Thursday night keg parties last night for Homecoming this weekend. I'm sorry."

"Oh yes, Homecoming. Well I hope you enjoy the basketball game and festivities. Do you know anyone coming?"

"Um, no. Well, maybe my sister. She lives on Long Island and said she might come up. Donna Reed is her old roommate and a good friend of hers."

"Oh sure, I know Donna, but I don't think I remember your sister. When did she graduate?"

"'76."

"Oh just before my time. I'm only here two years longer than you. I left the reading assignment written on the board for you. Please erase it after you write it down. Then please actually read it."

We laughed. "Have a good weekend, Professor."

"You too, Bob. I hope it's quiet."

For thirty-five years I've been staring at nineteen-year-olds and watched their disinterest grow more blatant to where they no longer attempt to hide their boredom, even their disdain, for class. For some time I took it personally until I understood most of them are having trouble putting all of these various moving parts together, understanding how they relate to their lives, their majors, and they often believe their only escape is to chat with childhood friends. And today the drinking age is twenty-one, so blowing off steam takes a bit more imagination.

So I welcomed Homecoming Weekend that February as a diversion. I hoped I'd see my sister but there was certainly no way of communicating at the time to know when or even if she planned to make the trip. My floormates would at the very least be on better behavior with parents hovering just across the street at the Castle Motel. I wandered out of Plassmann Hall and stopped to check my mail. Nothing. I stopped and talked to a close friend of mine headed toward another dorm who said her brother was down from Lockport and she would be hanging out with him that weekend. I started my climb up the echoing stairwell to Third West of Devereux Hall, passing students just waking up and headed out to class. A minute later I opened the door to my room, 327, to find my sister standing against my desk. And a beat later I looked at the person leaning against Steve's desk, and it was Joe Kohn. Deep tan, floppy leather hat, Dutch-cut blond hair, little round government issue glasses, and a smile as wide as campus, Joseph Lawrence Kohn.

"Hey," he said.

Everything changed.

Two

Antonio's

For thirty-five years I've been staring at nineteen-year-olds and one common denominator they all turn to for security is consistency . This makes sense. For the first eighteen years of their lives they, for the most part, had the predictable patterns and reliable expectations of home, parents, siblings, friends, neighbors. Suddenly, all bets are off. They don't know what to expect from their new neighbors, their new "parents" in the counseling, advising, and faculty communities all have questions for them they cannot yet answer, and even their home—a confined space equal in size to half their bedroom at home, is new and crowded with strangers. So finding a "new" routine, a new consistency, is necessary to ease their anxiety. In my day it was hanging out in someone's room drinking; today it might be some online game or long nights of streaming reels, or hours texting that friend from home they've known since first grade.

What is truly missing is a third place; somewhere they can go which is neither home nor school to escape the madness of all things new. In addition, they are in desperate need of some tangible diversion that pushes them out of their comfort zone. When I was young this came in the form of floormates heading for a hike or a drive into Canada. Or we walked to town and talked, pushed each other about our experiences, since absolutely no technological devices existed beyond a stereo in the dorm room or one television in the lobby with five or seven stations tops. Pulling college freshman out of their comfort zone today is a monumental task, so stuck are they in the same routine they've had since adolescence. Back then diversions were more readily available but uninteresting unless one drank, smoked pot, or studied. Since I had no consistency in my life anyway, I was open to suggestions.

Across from campus was a small Italian restaurant, Antonio's. It had two entrances: One on the left of the building for the lounge with the sunken bar where Dee the bartender served every night, and the main entrance on the right into the restaurant where a dozen or so tables filled the pleasant, small restaurant atmosphere. You could get from the lounge to the restaurant easily enough inside, but usually you entered one or the other from the parking lot. While their most popular dishes were pizza and wings, they remained true to their northern Italian origins with a full menu which drew people in from neighboring Olean, Hinsdale, and Allegany, New York. The more popular Castle Restaurant next door, attached to the Castle Motel and Castle Movie Theater, remained the dominant eatery, but Antonio's could draw the crowd with lesser means. The entire place was dimly lit enough for people to talk quietly, and the aroma of garlic and sauce seemed constant. I don't remember ever going there when there was more than one table available, and in the lounge, I could usually find professors having a drink to finish their day or a student or two having a beer to start their night.

Just a few days after his return to the United States and his drop-by with my sister to see me, Joe returned to campus to visit from his farm in North Collins, not an hour north of campus, and we walked across the street so he could once again have his favorite pizza after a four-year hiatus. Over the course of the next several months we spent many nights having pizza and wings; so often, in fact, that eventually the waiters and bartenders and cooks came to know us. This move from two guys having pizza to a veritable gathering was something I had never experienced before, and it filled this young freshman with some sense of adventure without ever leaving the college.

Joe talked about Africa or Brazil or answer my questions about his bike ride to South America, and people would just glance at this man with the floppy dirty blond hair with a Dutch cut, his dark, tanned skin in a Buffalo winter, his wide smile and little round glasses, and somehow feel welcome to join the conversation. Add to this energy the fact Joe loved to engage the server or the other customers with his always-ready quip, and before long, our table for two would be surrounded by chairs and engaged patrons.

This was weekly at the least. Twice a week more often, and once the planning started, even more than that.

It was a slow burn, this morphosis from a table for two to a veritable gathering. At first the server would stand at our table a bit longer, listen closely, and when she realized it was okay, she'd ask questions or make comments. This happened for several weeks as she came to know our names, that he was a grad and I was a freshman, that this had become my comfort zone. On slow nights she would pull up a chair, and after a few weeks when time slipped by and the kitchen had closed, the cooks would come out and join us. It wasn't long before I found myself making quips, exaggerating, laughing more easily, feeling lighter. It was as if for the first time life weighed nothing at all. Somewhere along the way, other customers would come in and listen, then comment, then join us. Regulars might automatically pull chairs up so that sometimes if a table for six was available, Joe and I would simply sit there knowing what was to come.

The professors who had been having a drink in the lounge would hear the laughter spilling in from the dining room and come to see what was going on. They soon joined us as well, often recognizing Joe as one of their former students, and I quickly was on a first name basis with philosophy and psychology profs, with priests, and with my own art teacher and friend, Cole, who Joe had been friends with when he was a student.

My mundane dorm life which so intimidated me because I had no desire to get drunk slipped from my consciousness as others—strangers at first—joined us for pitchers of beer just a hundred yards from Devereux Hall, and I sat intoxicated by stories of Africa, of Brazil. Couples invariably pulled their chairs to our table after Joe absorbed their conversation into ours. At the peak of this time, Friday and Saturday nights at Antonio's meant being surrounded by a dozen or more "friends" as we talked the night away. Joe talked about being an exchange student in Brazil and how he rode to South America by bike.

"I started at home near Buffalo," he told us, drawing a map on the back of a placemat. "I made it all the way to the Panamanian border, to the edge of the Darien Gap, but the forest was impenetrable, so I flew to Columbia and continued riding." He laughed hard and recounted how the spring before that trip he had crashed his motorcycle into a tree right in town and had fractured his leg in three places. The university doctor forbade him from walking for six weeks, minimum.

"What did you do?" a woman eating pasta at the next

table asked, sipping her wine poured from a bottle we all shared. She wasn't eavesdropping—no one ever was—Joe slid his presence into the path of anyone nearby.

"After four weeks I cut off my cast and rode out of town." He laughed hard again. "I averaged just twenty miles a day at first. But by the time I crossed the Mexican border, I kept a two hundred mile per day pace, dodged bottles thrown by passengers of passing cars and veered into ditches more than a few times." He said he didn't consider this ride an adventure, really. It was more an excuse to go away for a few months, and we all laughed. People bought us food, faculty joined us and treated me, just nineteen, like an equal, invited me into their world, a place Joe fit as easily as he did the South American highways. Everyone listened to his stories.

I had been terrified when I first moved from Long Island to Virginia, spending every day alone for three months while my parents worked, and then again when I arrived at campus and I anticipated another three months alone, scared to death to fit in where I knew no one, preferring instead to escape as I had before. But now, here, I found a place I not only felt comfortable—again—but somehow felt on the front edge of something I couldn't quite understand. This was the second time in my life I found myself this way, and both times the same person showed up with outrageous ideas. It has an impact.

Joe spoke of food in Africa and breakfasts in a Brazilian jail. "I met a woman on a bus near Belem," he said one night. "She gave me her name and number to call her if I needed anything. A few days later on another bus, I fell asleep, and somebody cut my bag away from my arm. I was arrested later that day for vagrancy.

"I called the lady for help," he continued, "but her

husband answered, and he was a cop and very jealous! He threatened to find me and beat me. The police let me leave so I could get out of town as quickly as possible." The next morning he took a boat up the Amazon to help start a fishery for former farmers he met in town who had been displaced by floods. While there, he traded his skills for their semi-precious gems. He carried home small bags of smoked and yellow topaz, uncut rubies, and various other stones. "They will help pay my way later," he said. At the time I didn't know what he meant. The conversation was always casual, like he was just answering the standard, "So, how was your day?" inquiry. It's just that his days were seemingly more interesting than ours.

Simply put, his stories tore a hole through my bored and irrelevant life, feeding some subtle ideas that lay dormant since I first met Joe when I was fifteen. His tales fed my imagination with oxygen, and something like hope finally rose to the surface. Plans I had abandoned suddenly clawed at my psyche. I had planned to ride my own bike across the country. I wanted to travel through Europe. I wanted to do a lot of things; but like a lot of things, my plans remained secondary to my situation—I was, after all, a college student with a smattering of interest in journalism on my way to a degree. But quite suddenly, sitting in the dimly lit Antonio's listening to Joe and feeling falsely more important simply by association, something seemed different, as if those plans of mine had been waiting for just the right spark to ignite their possibility, and they finally took on a life of their own.

Often, Joe talked about the Amazon, about the animals and people, and about how time disappeared there and left one clueless to the days, sometimes the seasons. People would ask about his "favorite" places, and he talked about the differences between Brazil and Zaire but more often noted the similarities, how they both seem to recede from the United States, and how the more advanced we become, the more the people in Zaire and Brazil appear fragile, more primitive, despite their competitive nature and drastic advances in the previous decades. Everyone listened with interest; I listened with intent. This was the early 1980's, before computers, cell phones, before Brazil woke like a sleeping giant, and before Zaire—now the Democratic Republic of the Congo—imploded from competition for precious minerals. Mostly, he liked talking about Zaire, about the people and their grasp on the immediate. "Conversations in my village lasted days. No one ran out of things to talk about despite having nothing to talk about," he'd joke. "Everyone here keeps jumping from topic to topic and can't keep still. How can you stand it?" he asked. He talked about the differences between so many things. He compared his bike trip to South America with my plan to cross the United States. We examined the different hobbies his friends had when he lived at college compared to those antics of my floor mates; how similar they were; how similar we were.

And, of course, he talked about the river. The Congo River.

He'd tell of how it winds and bends, and how the branches near Lumbumbashi cover the water like shrouds. The sun in the dry season shatters the surface and fish die or disappear. The woods are quiet in rural Zaire because many villagers believe spirits live there, and it's a good place for non-believers to get away, to be alone. He spoke of people in his village of Moma and their perspective of time, of how they have no concept of "later." If fruit on the vine isn't yet ripe, they'd still pick and eat it, even get sick, not understanding the value of waiting.

"It's like every day they wake up and are surprised," he joked.

He had respect for the villagers, their beliefs, and he had a sense of romance about the Congo. At Antonio's, Joe spoke of the river like a woman he once cared for and could not wait to see again, to recapture something they once shared. He described the area as what the world might have been like before humans marked time. Joe described the river itself as timeless, and he talked of it with the passion of a lover and the eyes of a writer. "Still," he said, "No one captured the atmosphere like Conrad." Joseph Conrad once wrote, "Going up that river was like traveling back to the earliest beginnings of the world, when vegetation rioted on the earth and the big trees were kings. An empty stream, a great silence, an impenetrable forest. The long stretches of the waterway ran on, deserted, into the gloom of overshadowed distances." Joe would quote *Heart of Darkness* like a missionary citing scripture and then spend hours clarifying for me the "overshadowed distances."

I felt that same sense of peace after a tumultuous first semester that I felt that first July in Virginia Beach after a distant and lonely June; that I'm not alone in my restlessness and boredom with the mundane. That Earth Science and Social Sciences have their place, but I didn't fit in; not yet anyway. I tried though, like all nineteen-year-olds, I tried to fit in, pretend I was interested, pretend I found it all so relevant and essential to my very existence, all the while feeling I belonged somewhere else. Always feeling slightly out of place, but close enough to fake it when I needed to.

But then this happened, these nights at Antonio's, the days walking along the river and talking about other places and the simple process of getting there, and I didn't need to pretend any longer. I sat among Joe and faculty and strangers at a small restaurant five hundred miles from where I grew up and felt completely at home.

Sometimes Joe just sat quietly and stared off, his mind abandoning western New York, wandering aimlessly amongst the villages near Lumbumbashi, Zaire's second largest city and eventual target of the Alliance of Democratic Forces for the Liberation of Congo-Zaire. Yet it is remote, with less than half a million poor, dying people. I mention the area today and people seem surprised anyone would think of traveling there. Rightly so. The Union for Democracy and Social Progress developed well there, though the local authorities jailed most of the members in the '80's. These rebels supported Zairian President Mobutu's programs, which opposition forces claim starved the country and drowned its progress. Yet these same opposition forces insisted on not receiving military help. They believed sending troops to the area might escalate fighting and lead to further death and "bloodletting." They were right. Later, in the '90's, Hutu militants who slaughtered villagers in Rwanda and Eastern Zaire would wander the streets. Some could be seen near Kolwezi manning gates and check points as early as the late eighties. But back in 1980 or so, it was peaceful, and on campus Joe would mentally wander its serene streets. Ethnic groups throughout Zaire traced roots to the region. It symbolized the source of many aspects of African life. But most notably for Joe, Lumbumbashi sat near the source of the Congo River.

And so it became a new routine that Joe split his time between home, my dorm room, and Antonio's. Eventually that would change as we moved our lives outside to the river, to the reservoir to the west, and to Niagara up north. He lived at home again surviving off his readjustment pay from the Peace Corps and a part time job he took at some canning factory. But to avoid being home all the time, he stayed at campus more frequently, sleeping on my dorm room floor, telling me stories until three or four in the morning. He felt at home. In fact, he told me once of all the places he had traveled in the world, he always felt most at home at St. Bonaventure. Still, the topic of nearly every conversation drifted toward Africa and I can't recall if I pushed him there or he went on his own and pulled me willingly along.

And sometimes late at night at Antonio's we added some new stories to the mix depending upon who was there to listen, like the night we were walking across campus and a friend of mine who I had a crush on called down from her second story dorm window. It was dark and she couldn't see well and said, "Holy Shit, are you John Denver??" Joe hesitated a second and replied, "I Am." I picked up on it immediately and said that "Mr. Denver" was on campus to see about doing a concert there, which was not out of realm of possibilities since I was deeply involved in coffeehouses and student activities by then. Of course, she didn't ask why we were wandering around at midnight, but his appearance won out. I said she'd get to meet him the next day. Of course, the next day came and "John" had to leave unexpectedly. Everyone at the table laughed loud and others in the restaurant turned around and within a short time our group grew.

I told them how we really did have a true John Denver encounter earlier that month when Joe and I, his brother Rick, and my friend Denise all went to Buffalo to a concert. The arena was set up in the round so that John Denver had to enter through the common hallway. As he waited to be announced onstage, we stood feet away on the other side of a small gate, and Joe said, "Hey John!" The singer turned to look just briefly but was visibly taken aback, laughed loud, threw his head back and said, "Far out!" just as he was called onstage.

Again, we slipped from that story into another, which bled to another, and on. It was simply like that all the time. It was a great way to be a freshman in college.

One night we walked across the street and the restaurant had some familiar faces. Strangely, Joe suggested we eat in the lounge, using that entrance, where the only other person was Dee and others wouldn't know we were there.

"Hey Bob, Joe. You not eating in the dining room?"

Joe answered. "No, just a quiet table in here tonight, Dee." And so we sat in the deep cushion, swivel chairs at a lounge table, and Dee brought peanuts and water. We ordered pizza. We talked about my classes, and I told him how bored I was, unable to stay focused for more than ten minutes sometimes. He laughed but was unusually quiet. I tried to shift the mood by mentioning my desire, still, to ride to Oregon one summer, and I asked him about his route to Brazil.

He clearly appreciated the question to have something to focus on, and when we finished eating, he turned over a place mat. On the back he penciled the Americas and outlined his bike trip, making sure the Pacific entered the canal further east than the Atlantic instead of further west, as most people think. He insisted on accuracy in the tomato-sauce details.

"When I got the plane ride across the pass into Columbia, we flew just above the trees the entire time. It was beautiful, Bob. I think that's what I love most about both the Congo and the Amazon; they're just beautiful." I ordered more wings and Dee brought them and retreated behind the sunken bar. Joe looked at the placemat and then looked at me. "I want to canoe the entire length of the Amazon. That's my plan," he said, putting down his pencil. I don't recall Joe using the word "dream." It was always "plan."

"Sounds dangerous," I said.

"Maybe, but not if I practice," Joe responded quite casually, reflectively, as if this had been well thought out for quite some time and I just became privy to an ongoing work-in-progress. My innocent image of Joe "practicing" for a canoe trip down the Amazon was of him paddling back and forth across the narrow Allegheny River; and he made it all seem that easy, like all adventurers and explorers make their plans seem that easy. I always remembered a particular exchange that night when, jokingly, I said, "Well, just do your best," and laughed. He laughed as well and said, almost as a throwaway, "I will try, especially since nobody ever knows what their best is, they just decide they've done their best when they get tired or bored."

That stayed with me. For thirty-five years I've asked nineteen-year-olds to write a few hundred words about being in college. "Do your best," I tell them. They write the paragraph, and I ask them if they had the chance to take another shot at it, but this time I would give automatic A's for the semester to the five that make me sit up, how many would do better, and universally they all admit that, yes, they would do better. I push them one further: I tell them that the student who writes the one paragraph that really captures my attention will receive five thousand in cash, and then I ask how many would do better on the paragraphs then and they all laugh and say of course they would, as if I just asked the most insane question. I wait a beat, then I say, "So, you just admitted it, didn't you?" They stare at me perplexed. "You just admitted that you always could have done better, you just couldn't be bothered. Not until someone paid you." I let that sink in, then I tell them never again to tell anyone they're doing their best, because more likely than not, they're not doing their best at all. What they're doing, I tell them, is constructing their own glass ceilings.

It was winter in Western New York, and outside Antonio's a cold fog settled into the valley from the hills to the north, toward Buffalo, and to the south across the fields behind campus sat a fog so thick we could no longer see the hills beyond the Allegheny River. Inside where it was warm and the aroma of garlic drifted to the lounge from the kitchen, we sat quietly a bit longer, and then Joe moved my empty plate and glass, flipped over my placemat, and drew another map using blue cheese from the wings and tomato sauce from the pizza, making curvy lines with a knife. I sat back and watched the hazy vagueness become clearer, like a photograph in a dark room or a reoccurring dream. It took a while and a bit of agitating for the image to reveal itself.

Sauce splattered the place mat, and Joe sat upright, his eyes darted to me, then to the mat as he drew slowly, and he smiled and nodded. At first, I thought he drew the Amazon, but it looked kind of like New York or Virginia. He carefully covered the entire sheet then drew a line with blue cheese dressing to resemble a highway running from the southeast in a bell-curve, back down to the southwest.

"Brazil?" I asked.

"Zaire." He pointed to the blue cheese. "That's the Congo River."

"I have an idea," he said, and very quickly the mat sat stained with symbols of borders and rivers. The sketch of the Congo River stretched from Lumbumbashi across the equator twice to Banana Beach on the Atlantic.

"I'm going to canoe the Congo River. No one in history has ever done this alone."

"Not the Amazon?" I asked.

"I don't know the Amazon like I do the Congo. This really is just practice," he said, laughing. Then, more seriously, he added, "We need to figure this out."

We asked Dee for a pen and paper but all he had were bar napkins, and within a few hours they were filled with lists upon lists of things to get, people to contact, activities to learn, all composed in the course of the night. Eventually, Dee locked up and we stood to leave.

Outside in the foggy, cold night, the entire campus across the road was quiet, and we stopped walking under the restaurant sign. "Bob, I need your help," he said in almost a whisper, as if all the other people we ever met were somehow listening in and he didn't want anyone else to hear.

I stood up straighter. Something relevant was finally about to happen; something interesting and somehow necessary. My life stood up. My very being and existence stood at attention, as if I finally learned to breathe on my own.

Three

Fly

One afternoon on our way out of my dorm room, Joe walked into a room on my floor where some upper classmen lived; drinkers who made it a point to try and get me drunk or exclude me entirely when I refused, feeling superior for the efforts; yet I no longer cared. Joe walked in and one of them asked what he wanted.

"I used to live here." He looked around. "I had a refrigerator over there and a cabinet. I ran a sub shop. I made some good money too! Until they shut me down!" We all laughed, and we talked for an hour. One of the guys asked why he was shut down. "I guess I was too much competition for the café!"

When sober, they weren't so bad.

This seems more of a childish recollection than any sort of character development, but the significance lies in the previous six months of absolute ridicule, teasing, and exclusion. I handled it the entire time by ignoring the comments or disappearing completely. I mastered the art of disappearance. It was easy in the early eighties to cut yourself off from civilization. The payphone rarely worked so communication with folks back home was sporadic at best, and it didn't take long for my parents to understand

I wouldn't be calling. I had already lost touch with most of my high school friends since we were still fifteen years from handheld devices—even the cordless phone was not yet available. It was quite common then, that after my Thursday classes when I didn't need to be anywhere except possibly the radio station until the following Tuesday morning, I might just up and leave without telling anyone since no one noticed anyway. That's not being self-analytical; it was the same for us all then. "He probably took off for the weekend" was said about anyone who couldn't be found. Sometimes I only went as far as the hills behind campus, sometimes only to a friend's room in another dorm. Occasionally, when I could borrow a car, I'd head up to Niagara. My first semester in college left me exhausted for the sheer amount of time I was either in defense mode or simply taking off to anywhere.

I never quite adjusted to dorm life. These new companions live with you, closer than your siblings, and you're now vulnerable, self-conscious, and anxiety ridden. You share a bathroom with ninety guys and nothing about your life is a secret anymore. When you're not in your tiny dorm room, your roommate is and so are his friends, often drunk, high, or going through your stuff—at at least that's what you figure is happening, and it probably is.

Your sleep pattern is different than it ever was for your first nineteen years, and different from one night to the next. Two hours sleep might be enough, and it certainly can be a lot given fire alarms, the two-a.m. return from closing pubs, or the keg parties outside your door. You adjust little by little, grow up a lot, and everything in life is brand new, unexplored water, and you paddle through it cautiously, waiting, completely expecting, to capsize at any given moment. But you survive and you have new friends and a new routine, and at night you meet in the skellar, or The Club in town to shoot pool and get a pitcher or two.

Or you're me, and you go for walks along the trails or borrow someone's car and drive to Canada, bored, failing, and absolutely certain you're just one thought away from figuring it all out. But, of course, you never do. You just learn when to study, when to shower, when to avoid certain floormates and when to confront them; and when you figure it out, it will change again. And you know you've been pegged as the uncool one, the different one, the pathetic one who should have stayed in the south. They tolerate you because you're a musician; they despise you because you don't play The Clash.

Then, on a dime, that changed.

My floormate Tim introduced himself to Joe. Joe replied, "I'm Fly."

"Fly?"

When Joe was a student, someone bet him he couldn't scale the outside of the dorm to the fourth floor. He took the challenge and everyone waiting in line at the dining hall next door watched as he worked his way up the bricks moving from windowsill to water pipe. "He looks like a fly!" someone shouted. And so it was. In art class he would even draw a fly instead of writing his name. He had fun with it all, majoring in psychology and minoring in popularity. No one in my dorm could ignore his presence, his dark tan in winter and his floppy hat, his enthusiasm, his energy, and his attitude. By association, they could not ignore me. But it was something more than that; I could never relate to the evenings my floormates spent drinking. Now I felt like I didn't have to.

We stayed for an hour, talking and joking; Joe mentioned my bike trip, his canoe journey. At the end he asked if they wanted to join us that weekend for a hike up in Ontario. They declined but seemed at the least interested, more probably intrigued. We left.

Suddenly I fit it just when I no longer felt like I needed to.

Sometime later when I asked professors if they knew of Joe Kohn, they hesitated. But when I said, "Fly," it was clear his reputation endured. At basketball games he would swirl a Brazilian blanket around his head when we scored, and after the game, students, alumni he knew, and faculty, even priests, stood by to talk, and I stood there too, somehow a host, a vicarious adventurer. Inevitably, we moved the conversation to Antonio's, laughing and talking in a group across the front lawn of campus, across Route 417, into the dining room where we stayed all night, all of us.

We were rarely alone. Students would come and go from my room when they heard Joe around, and they'd listen to his stories. When he was up at the farm, everyone wanted to know where he was. It didn't take long for my room to become communal, and everyone had questions, which just motivated Joe to tell more outrageous stories. His energy was addicting and spilled out of the room and brought everyone to life, and we all felt alive. It was quite simple, in retrospect. We were all terrified of college; we didn't know what to expect at any stage of the game, even those of us with older siblings who had already been through it. These years are an ongoing mystery. But here was a man who chased his plans to the far reaches of the planet, who had once lived right here, down the hall to the left, just like us. This made whatever's next seem more doable. Joe appeared as a safe passage from the unspoken fears of life as it was to the terrifying mystery of life to come.

These young men today run companies, litigate supreme court trials, host the evening news, make international trades equal to my lifetime income, and raise families. They're good guys who at one time were as lost as I was, but we all managed to keep it a secret from each other.

When it was just the two of us again in my room, he pulled a box out of his pack. It was filled with malachite hearts, pendants, small malachite heads and eggs, and rough stones. Hundreds of them covered the floor, some dark with even lines marking their high value, other slighter, swirling with poor quality. Small ivory rings filled small photo containers, and in his car he carried several five and six feet long carved ivory tusks, brought back before the ban. Next to him he opened a tin filled with rubies, topaz, and a few aqua marines.

"We have to sell these," he said, "to help pay for the trip." He gave me a pad and we noted the numbers of each, the cost, what he wanted for them.

The next day we drove to the mall in town and walked from kiosk to kiosk, him with some satchels of jewels, me with a bag of malachite hearts, and both of us with long ivory tusks on our shoulders. We attracted attention, but by now I was quite used to it.

Several young women bought jewels and hearts, and one man walking out of a jewelry store stopped to admire the topaz, bought a few, and was studying the tusk on my shoulder when security came. We had made more than five hundred dollars, and security was not happy. At first, they wanted to confiscate the items, but instead just took our ID's, wrote down our names, and told us to leave the mall and never come back for any reason.

When we returned to the dorm and he readied to leave, he gave me the tin filled with jewels and hearts and asked me to sell them after he left and send the money to a friend of his in Kinshasa.

This education beyond freshmen comp and sociology became clear; yet I also noted how they fed each other, the experiences with Joe demonstrated how important those courses are, and my growing desire to learn, to prepare for the trip as if it was *my* trip and mine alone, lit a spark in me to experience anything I could. We drove to Niagara Falls and talked to people from all over the world. We would head to a local pancake house at three a.m. and laugh about mishaps in Brazil, villagers in Zaire, family in North Collins. I was learning to take chances, to enjoy the moment, and to unapologetically be myself. As close as I had become to my writing instructors at the college, in the only classes that kept my attention, it was these outings filled with laughter and stories where I found the motivation to keep going., Something was desperately lacking in the classroom—not in small part because faculty simple didn't talk much about it, and some probably had no real-world experience at all to be in a position to communicate it.Relevance. I was learning to make connections between classroom material and life.

For thirty-five years I've stared at the confused stares of nineteen-year-olds when I discuss, for instance, process writing. "When will I ever need to write a process paper, ever in my life?" they ask, much as I did to Dr. Brisbane my freshman year. His answer was "for starters, Mr. Kunzinger, right now," and that was the end of it . That pissed me off because I really wanted to know, so I tell my students, "I know; you want relevance. Well, I'll tell you, the skills of a simple process paper, which in and of itself seems so irrelevant to you, include learning to understand how to make something work, but more importantly a paper like this will teach you what to include and what to leave out, how to anticipate problems, how to avoid them, how to correct them if something goes wrong anyway. These are some of the best skills you'll ever know, all in a stupid little process paper."

I don't tell them I had the same response when I was their age. But relevance redefined my collegiate life. From this point on every class came with my complete understanding of how I could use the material.

After marking the list of all the jewels and ivory, we walked to his car he had parked near the old friary on campus. A priest walked by and said hello. Joe stepped to him and introduced himself.

"I'm Joe."

"Fr. Alphons Trebold. Are you an alumnus?"

"I am," he replied. "Your name sounds French," Joe said, and the two spoke in French for a while. "I'm getting ready to head to Africa for a trip."

"Well that sounds exciting," Father said, and gave Joe a quick blessing a la St. Francis of Assisi. The college was founded by Franciscans. "And you know, gentlemen, that Bonaventure means 'good travel.'" He continued on his way.

Joe left and I walked along the river back to the dorm, taking my time under a star-filled sky. I thought of the constellations we studied which sit above The Congo, and I laughed to myself at how my Astronomy professor seemed confused by my sudden interest in the stars and my endless stream of questions. The same thing happened in my psychology class when I turned a C- into an A and asked about tempering loneliness, dealing with extreme isolation. How small the world suddenly seemed; how much more I felt somehow aware of life around me, like I had always been staring but never seeing, and someone finally arrived who could show me what to look for. I wondered how many of us at that age are just looking in the wrong direction or don't even know what we should be looking for to begin with. Teachers today ridicule students for not paying attention, or not asking the right questions, or staring at their phones. It's all true but we need to learn to make excuses for them. More likely than not, they haven't the foggiest idea what questions to ask, and the phone is more than likely a safe zone they turn to when it all gets too much to understand. That phone just might keep them from crashing and dropping out.

The following weekend Joe found me in the café, sat down, and said, "I don't know what I'm going to do without you over there!" and laughed. He meant it, but he also meant it in a way of reminding me he appreciated all we'd been through. "I'll have to talk to the crocs!" he laughed. I thought of Joseph Conrad who wrote, "There was no shadowy friend to stand by my side in the night of enormous wilderness." *Which ingredient dispels loneliness*, I thought.

Once, not long before he left, we drove to his farm in North Collins. His youngest sister, Kim, was there, only five or so, and he held her for a bit before we headed further up to Buffalo to attend a John Denver concert with his brother Rick. After the concert on the way home he was unusually quiet for a bit, and I asked why, what was he thinking about. "My sister," he said. "And my brothers. I want to spend more time with them when I get back."

"You mean before the Amazon trip?" I asked, laughing.

"Yes, right before then!"

The expression, "It's a world away from here" was never more apt than when I spent my days studying the dangers as well as the potentials of one of the most untouched places in the world, and my nights at concerts, stopping for pancakes at three in the morning. *This could not be the normal routine of a college student*, I thought. But I quickly realized I already tried normal. It didn't work out .

Four

Education

For thirty-five years I've stared at nineteen-year-olds, and I see a common trait to this day; they don't see why they need most of the material they are assigned. Many never learn the difference between a higher education and a certificate program, and as a result many are misplaced. Along the way, however, teaching in a military town has enriched my classrooms with active-duty and retiring military personnel who have already experienced the world more than many people probably ever should, and they return to the classroom with a newborn understanding and appreciation of relevance. It is what I call their "Time of Clarity," when everything eventually makes sense. Nothing seems to make much sense at nineteen when, ironically, so many people want you to have all the answers to your life's plans. It is only the retiring forty-year-old back from her second tour who can say with absolute frankness, "I have no idea." That's when education starts.

For instance:

It was about 1994. Student comes to see me. He says he can't handle the pressure of school. I tell him I think he's a good student and he says yes, he can do the work, he just can't stand it. He hates it, he says. He gets bored fast. It's a good conversation, honest. Had we been somewhere else we would have talked over beers. He immediately reminds me of me before Joe and I planned the Congo trip. He looks at his watch and says he has to work in a few hours and sighs. He's twenty-five and runs his own roofing company but hates that too. He has six grand invested in equipment and no help and he just dreads doing the work now. He says he's at some fork in the road, referencing our work in class, two paths that look the same, so he's frozen, finds it easier to just stay put. He gets quiet and stares at a photograph on my wall of a village in Africa. Looks nice he says, like he wants to say anything to forget what he's really thinking about. Then he remembers and sighs again. He's quiet for some time and I find myself drifting.

I worked at a bar. Good money and mindless work; the kind of work where if you don't think too much about what you're doing, you can keep on working. I know I only spent a few years there, but it seems like it was always winter, all grey and bone-cold. One morning I woke on a bench near a lake in a park and didn't know how I got there. I had to work a few hours later but never made it. I quit the bar, withdrew most of my money, and bought a ticket to Africa. Turns out changing my life was as easy as jumping off a cliff knowing for certain I would either land on my feet or learn how to fly.

But this student has trouble talking about it, so I talk: I tell him I get that feeling in my chest too. Tight, constricting, difficulty breathing. You know what I'm talking about. It's the sense that something needs to change. I tell him all of that, and then I think, but I don't say, it's the Philosophy class with five minutes left of three hours and the prof starts another chapter because there are still five minutes left; it's the meeting you can't tolerate but you're in a row of seats with too many people on both sides so you can't leave and all you can think about is how if this is your career, if this is how you've chosen to spend your life, shouldn't you love being here, love the interaction and discussions instead of dreading every word that someone says; it's that this-homily-is-way-too-long feeling. It's the feeling you're just one day away from something else, but then that day comes, and you find yourself one day away from something . I tell him it's the Whitman poem about astronomy; the wide awake at three am feeling and you can't move so you stare at the alarm clock wondering what your someday-dying self would say to you now.

Exactly, he says. I'm always staring at the clock. I'd love to know what you'd do, he says. I tell him about a bar somewhere I didn't belong. I remember working and then not working but I don't remember what happened between the two. I just recall waking up one day in the peace-of-mind of another world, centuries away from being behind bars; like I could finally breathe on my own. I remember dreading the moment between what was and what was next, so I just kept pouring drinks, hesitating, putting off change. But then one day I didn't, and when I looked back from where I ended up, the "what used to be" that so engulfed my life didn't even exist anymore. He looks at me like I am looking in a mirror. I tell him if it were me, I'd withdraw from school, liquidate my roofing equipment, put some in the bank and some in the gas tank and keep just one slice of life to myself for a while. School isn't going anywhere, I tell him. We'll wait for you.

He stares at me a long time then laughs, sweeps his long blond hair back and blinks his eyes a few times, as if to restrain some emotion. "I'm not that brave," he says, and we laugh. Then he says he's going to work and he leaves.

Six months later he sends me this postcard from Australia. "Don't know when I'll return," it says. "When I am, let's get some beers and talk." I look forward to it but, of course, way leads on to way, and I doubt he ever came back.

Little in life motivates us more than relevance, and when we can't find it, our brain cells have trouble processing any reason to do anything at all. But when we do recognize the hidden reasons behind a project, that illusive internal motivation springs to life. One thing finally became clear to me; I could use this material they're teaching; I finally found a reason to learn. And from then on I was constantly learning. In class I sat up with the enthusiasm of an honors student and after class I moved about with a confidence borne of the bend Joe applied to his plans—stop thinking about it and go. I stayed after class to clarify material; I went early to ask questions. Some professors could not know the reason for my sudden passion, but a few did, and they would sometimes ask if Joe and I were going to be at Antonio's that night and said that they might stop by. They often would. This was early proof to me of a concept which would play a significant role in my life much later as a professor: Even the faculty know the best education is not solely in the classroom and not solely in the world, but an absolute blending of both, ideally feeding off of each other, with the student spiraling up, spinning through classes and continents, textbooks and train stations.

Part of that experience included the lesson that failure and quitting needed to be foreign ideas, non-existent, success in this case could only be achieved through meticulous planning and constant training. We bought a stopwatch and turned the canoe over on each other, timing our speed to shore ahead of imagined crocs and hippos. "Hippos are fast!" Joe said and flipped me once more. The water was shallow near campus, so we drove to Lake Chautauqua an hour west. We knew this part of planning was pure "folly," but not if one considers those particular aspects of our days to be a dose of morale, a systematic shot of confidence. We camped in the hills on cold nights and made fires from sticks and leaves, hoping farmers didn't care. We never gave up despite rain, frosts, and cowherds. Everything naturally bent toward completion and success. The literature department became an afternoon cocktail hour, teachers humming about, listening to stories of Africa and South America. Faculty marked the differences between Hemingway's stories and those Joe told, asking him to speak in classes, insisting we all go to dinner that evening and talk further. We all took this as a chance to escape the confines of the small western New York town, albeit briefly. Yet I felt separate from it all, more part of the journey than the professors who joined the conversation, yet not quite part of "our" trip as Joe and I pretended I was. No, I spent much of this time dangling in the between, one foot in class, the other in the Congo; half of my attention on journalism, the rest on distant places I suddenly knew better than anyone else on campus yet didn't know at all. It was an odd place to be, and in it I learned too well how to pretend everything was fine.

We discussed writers and truths and fables and poetry over dinner and dessert. Every meal included discussions of food. Potatoes and leeks can be produced in the high plains of the east and south. The cool temperatures and fertile soil of the Eastern Highlands favor the cultivation of tomatoes, sweet potatoes, yam and pumpkins. Even Mediterranean vegetables such as artichokes and asparagus can thrive. The agricultural yield could be so high that it wasn't uncommon during the rainy season to replant immediately after harvest and get a second crop before the same season ended.

But none of that happens anymore. "The government in charge abandoned its responsibilities, and no one else knows what to do," Joe told the political science prof. Since the 1960s, agriculture has been seriously neglected and at times the government allocated to it as little as only one percent of its total budgetary spending. The 1973-1974 nationalization or "Zairianisation" of most small and medium-size foreign-owned agricultural enterprises had a disastrous effect on production, which never recovered. Now, subsistence farmers make up about eighty percent of the DRC's population. They're sharecroppers. Fish could be a valuable source of food but remains another under-exploited sector with huge potential. The lakes in eastern and southern regions are a massive reserve of a variety of freshwater species, such as the Tilapia. The Congo River is another important source with major fishing ports in Kisangani and Mbandaka supplying the six million people living in Kinshasa.

The astronomy professor let us sit in on classes where we learned about reading the night sky above equatorial Africa. It was then I knew the level my new dedication to learning had reached; I was sitting in on classes I did not need to attend.

The sociology prof always asked about different aspects of infrastructure, explaining how knowing where to find things, including friendly people, can often be predicted based upon highways and communication towers. But Joe was quick to point out that in the Congo the river is the interstate and more easily traveled than the dilapidated roads, even in the capital. Professor Shepard supported that and asked leading questions about how you can find food and help based upon often primitive infrastructure. In Kinshasa, the highways aren't any better now than they probably were when Henry Stanley founded the city. Trying to truck in food and supplies is disastrous on the poor road infrastructure, so fishing remains the primary means of survival for much of the nation, but citizens can't even manage that because of politics. "It's said," Joe commented once over pizza, "that the Congo is the only place fish die of old age."

We talked about culture in Africa, and history and bones in Africa. Joe spoke of modern adventurers who attempted to navigate the rivers, not knowing the landscape, not understanding the languages. Even nearby villagers would die of starvation or disease, he'd say. What made these migrant people from another hemisphere think they could conquer the territory? For Joe it was easy: He didn't consider himself an outsider, but instead an adopted son, taken in by villagers as one who should have been born there and so called it his home and the people his friends.

One day in the hallway of a classroom building while talking to a philosophy professor, I stood and watched Joe interact not unlike he must have when he was still a psychology major here. I thought about his return from the Peace Corps with no set plans, and I wondered if this trip of ours was a way for him to return to school, carry on where he left off and where he was happiest.

In the campus biology labs, where the odor of formaldehyde reeked, we learned natural cures and homeopathic medicine. We studied with marked frustration the causes and symptoms of diseases, intestinal and other. So many diseases had similar, even identical, symptoms, and we learned quickly how easy it is to die on the Congo. Malaria could be a flu or could be dehydration or could be the beginning of Ebola. Even a small case of diarrhea which could lead to worms, one biology professor reminded us, could spell death if not attended to. Quiz upon quiz from medical guides and State Department fliers became leisure reading. Joe and I managed to master the names and uses of plants, their medicinal value, their tastes. Hibiscus leaves soaked in the sun made fine tea. Luckily, Joe's years in the region rendered some of the learning redundant, but studies were necessary. We became astronomers, noting the charts of stars along the central African equator. We memorized weather patterns and atmospheric conditions. On a calendar I noted the start and end of rainy seasons. We anticipated when the following year's rain would come, guessing with a two-week grace period either way. At the Political Science department, we studied the relationships among surrounding countries such as Angola, the Central African Republic, Rwanda, Kenya and others. Zaire is huge and is the heart of what had always been known as "the Dark Continent." When the State Department maps arrived, we marked the route, considered the time it would take to travel between villages to restock food and contact friends in Kinshasa if he had to.

We stood in the library at an old wooden table, a few students and a couple of librarians with us. "The Lualaba River is the vein through which I will enter the river region, heading toward the Congo." He pointed with a pencil to the Lualaba on the map. "This will be my primary route until after Kolwezi."

"Why not just start at the actual Congo?" someone asked.

"Well, it is the Congo, kind of. The source of the Congo is near Lumbumbashi, and the river down there has several names. Luaba and Lualaba are just two." Names in Africa, particularly in the 1970's, kept changing, the result of colonialism followed by independence. The country's name, Zaire, for instance, was derived from the name of the Congo River, sometimes called Zaire in Portuguese, which in turn was derived originally from the Kikongo word nzere or nzadi, meaning "the river that swallows all rivers." In 1997, the country's name was changed again to the Democratic Republic of Congo, though the river, sometimes during this time called "the Zaire," was always and always would be simply Congo.

Joe needed to navigate his way to the Congo River from its origin to justify, in his mind, doing the entire "river" alone. "The Congo doesn't begin in earnest until well into the country, though villagers call all of the tributaries flowing north from Lumbumbashi into the main river 'The Congo,'" he added, and everyone seemed satisfied. Even Joe seemed satisfied. I was starting to recognize subtle signs of false confidence, of hesitant certainty.

The unspoken reality for everyone from the server at Antonio's to the professors and librarians to me, and even to Joe, was just how dangerous this journey truly is. Some planning revealed obvious concerns. For instance, Joe didn't carry any guns, for this might suggest he was a mercenary. Just before he left, several government officials disappeared in south central Zaire, west of Bukavu. Embassy reports blame rebels from Uganda, where invaders attacked the Shaba province on two occasions. "If they hadn't been carrying guns," one report stated, "they might still be alive. It is assumed they were soldiers." But to not carry guns is not smart.

"How do you avoid such dangers?" Cole asked, a man who was the first and closest friend to both Joe and me of all the professors and had no trouble cutting through the fat to get to the bone of a situation. "Seriously," he said. "The real question must be, the entire time you guys are mapping out this trip of yours, is how do you do this without dying?"

"The reality is," I said, talking to the others but looking at Joe, "the only insurance against dying is to not travel at all. How do you know things haven't changed over there in the past year? News out of the Congo doesn't exactly flow into Cattaraugus County, New York. And how do you know you'll remember everything from when you lived there?"

"Hell, we can all die just crossing the road here back to campus!" We all laughed, but I never understood such comparisons, like "it's safer to fly than it is to drive." The statistics are skewed, the question is flawed. Where are the stats of people in car accidents who survived compared to the people in plane crashes who survived? Of course it is safer to drive, based upon "chance," not deceptive calculations; it's a non-comparison. There are no crocs on Route 417 in Allegany, New York. No rebels or warring villagers. There is no schistosomiasis or Ebola in the rivers of Cattaraugus County.

So, yes, we talked about death. Of course. But death is not always the worst thing that can happen to someone, and it is certainly not the worst fate that can happen to someone you care about. We never anticipated missing. It simply never crossed our minds.

Five

Language

Joe and I walked behind campus along the old railroad tracks covered by weeds and fallen trees.

"Fish?" Joe asked.

"Mbisi."

"Good. And in Swahili?"

"Samaki."

"Snake?"

"Lingala or Swahili?"

"Both."

"Nyoka... Actually, nyoka for both, right?"

He smiled and nodded. "Blood?"

"Makila in Lingala and damu in Swahili. Why do you need to know how to say blood?"

"Good. River?"

"Ebale and Mto. Why do you need to know how to say blood?"

The practice wasn't for me. I was never going to have to speak either Lingala or Swahili. I did not yet know, of course, that would change. Still, at the time I knew some French, but even then, when the trip was done and I flew to Kinshasa to meet Joe out at Banana Beach, the mouth of the Congo at the Atlantic, I'd be with someone who spoke

English, so these daily quizzes were to help Joe remember the languages during these months he was home. He insisted he learned more by helping me to learn than just by reading.

"You did great!" Joe said.

"Asante Mengi."

"Karibu! Now, hebu tula!" Let's eat. That one I knew.

"What's the word for pizza?"

"There is none."

"Uncivilized!" I said, and we laughed our way to Antonio's.

"Let's talk about animals," Joe said with too much excitement for the context of our discussion.

Our server seemed disappointed at first. "Animals? I'll sit this one out tonight, guys," she laughed. Two other tables of familiar faces pulled their chairs to our table like it was afterhours at a wedding reception when most of the guests have gone home.

"Animals play important roles, and each creature is identified with a particular trait. The antelope or gazelle represents intelligence, the pig is considered foolish, the lion stands for strength, and the crocodile is usually a villain. Honestly, this is important if you want to relate to the villagers."

"Why?" someone once asked, sipping his wine, tie undone, staying far later than he must have planned.

"I'll be stopping in villages along the river for food and other possible supplies, and they need to know I understand their culture. If it comes up."

"You gotta respect the crocs," he laughed.

And so on weekends we'd wade into the Allegheny River to our knees or head to Chautauqua, or the lake at the state park, and he'd call to me, "I never met one that had enough to eat!"

From a vantage of ten thousand miles away, I became a student of Africa. I discovered local Congolese folklore and the legends and tales of each ethnic group, which though separated by language and culture, all share certain characteristics. We saturated the evenings in the library or the ministry center or the dorm lounge with literature. We concentrated on pre-twentieth century material, mostly by or about explorers, but recent writings intrigued us as well. After the Second World War, a large body of literature developed, written in French, local Bantu languages and, in some cases, Flemish (a language spoken in Belgium and so carried to the Congo). Two of the region's best-known writers are Antoine Roger Bolamba, who was not only an important poet but also the author of sociological and folklore studies, and V.Y. Mudimbe, who has published poetry, criticism and several novels, beginning in 1973 with *Between the Tides*, in which the protagonist discovers a whole new way of seeing the world. We talked about translation, laughed over misinterpretation of words, and realized the dangers in trying to communicate. It was my time between the tides of my youth, of childish high school ways, and this sudden thrust into not just adulthood, but into an arena on an international scale. The first bar I faced in college turned out to be set pretty high as we studied everything we could so he could make this solo journey on one of the most dangerous rivers in the world in one of the most remote regions. I joked with him once that I apparently had never been asked to think before. He said that thinking for class and investigating for life are two different animals. He sounded like my journalism profs who often pointed out the need for real-life research for even the smallest of ideas. It was a whole new way of seeing the world.

"See why you're taking etymology classes?" he asked,

just a few weeks after I had complained about the required Greek and Latin etymology for journalism students.

"None of the...Joe, not one of the languages I'm quizzing you about have any relationship at all to either Greek or Latin!"

"How's your French?" I was quiet and smiled.

"Remember, you'll be in Kinshasa in about a year!"

"Oui," I said, laughing. "Now, hebu tula." We talked continually while eating, and many of those conversations were, in fact, about food. Each of our meals included a discussion about breakfast, about dinner, about finding food in the jungle, in the mountains, about trading for food in villages, and about water, its deadly saturation and its deadly absence. And we tried to converse in other languages, albeit only one word here and one word there. Still, my grades in etymology drastically improved. Relevance. I took a sip of ice water and thought about how I didn't have to think about it. But on the Congo, water is oxygen; it carries you where you need to go, yet it can flood villages forcing them upland just when you might need sustenance and the stop you planned to make is no longer available, so you continue on without water or food, and dehydration from the absolute lack of clean water can kill. I had never been so aware of every sip of water, and I was more aware of when I wasn't drinking water, wasn't studying. For the first time in my life, I became acutely aware of when I *wasn't* learning something.

We listened to music. My floor mates played Stray Cats, The Doors, The Dead, and The Ramones. I played Warren Zevon and the music of griots. In some pedestrian way, griots are the village historians and genealogists as they sing about fishing, planting, or the river. They sing to alleviate the tedium of work. Joe had carried home tapes of this music, and I listened while he translated, told stories of villagers he knew, "family" he called them. "You can tell a lot about a group of people standing around just by listening to the music they might be playing. So before I open my mouth, I know which language to use, what customs to avoid, whether I should engage or not." Another lesson learned: Remain silent until you understand your surroundings.

We got back to the dorm one night to the smell of beer drifting down the stairwell and the sound of music pouring through the doors. I stood in the hallway in the late-night/early morning hours and listened to the music of these villagers on my floor, and I wanted little part of it all. I had no interest in partying or their pursuit of a good time. I suppose I felt above that, which was certainly arrogant as well as somewhat immature and judgmental, but I simply never fit in to begin with. So when the options were a dorm party where the names of those who threw up were written on the walls, or a drive to Niagara Falls to talk about what it was like to bike through Guatemala and what I could expect on a trip west, I believe I won. In the end, Joe's arrival didn't "save" me from a college dorm-life I despised as much as it allowed me to remain in the thick of college life, but on my own terms. Eventually, we all got along well. I listened to their music, joined them in the rathskeller for beers and wings, but they never really understood my indifference to it all, and to be fair neither did I, not completely. I always seemed to say the wrong thing. Well, that's probably because my floormates and I never spoke the same language.

So Joe and I studied the similarities of Lingala, Lomongo, Kikongo, Kiswahili and other Bantu derivatives.

More importantly, we discussed when to speak and when not to speak a particular language. Those who speak Congolese fight with those who speak Lomongo. Villagers speak Kiswahili in the east. Lingala is used more now than it was then, but then it was still used more than Kikongo. African borders reflect colonial history rather than linguistic boundaries, so many languages are spoken in one area. Some Congo languages use tones. In the river region, for instance, some languages only count to five, and the other numbers are derivatives of that. Six, for instance, is five plus one. Some villagers rely upon click language, using fifteen click consonants borrowed from South African languages. We found out the political reasons for this, which led us to the Political Science department. Villagers fight over land use, over river use. Villagers fight over religion and money. The government controls the fighting by feeding whichever faction most favors their objectives and whichever group of people has the most influence in the region. We learned the province names, the origin of customs. I knew more about central African life than I did my own, and the notion that this was "Joe's trip" seemed to slowly slip away as both Joe and I began to say, "Our maps," "our raft," "our health."

"Our trip." We reached a point where I absolutely forgot I wasn't going.

My life was never so clarified. On the surface, it had to be a solo trip simply because it had never been done solo at the time. Furthermore, I was not mentally prepared. Seriously, by the time of the trip I had just turned twenty; I didn't even want to tell my parents about riding to Oregon, forget about mentioning a year long journey on The Congo River. Even had my family given me permission to travel to remote Africa, it was not on my radar anyway. For me, it was just a training period. I learned as an apprentice might;

I served my internship for adventure with a modern David Livingstone. I sat as a passenger, an observer of the journey. I had other plans; this is what I tried to convince myself.

And one night quite late after Antonio's had closed, we sat in the college ministry center on chairs staying warm from the chill coming down from Lake Erie. It was well past midnight, and my roommate was asleep, so we left. Joe and I walked along the river, waded across to the hills on the other side and hiked to the clearing where Merton used to sit and write in his journal. We returned and sat inside the ministry center named for the monk, with our wet shoes and socks off, and Joe told me in the most detail yet of the journey, of what the river was like—its wideness and narrowness, its isolation and commerce, its stagnancy and current. He looked right at me a few times as was his way, but mostly he looked out the window, almost forcing me to look out there as well toward the library and classroom buildings nearby, but also past them, past the borders and populations, toward some remote place deep in some darkness not yet visible. I glanced that way a few times half-expecting to see fishermen, villages, and wildlife. Joe grew up on a dairy farm right there in western New York and had lived in Africa practicing animal husbandry in a small village in Zaire. His details were filled with enough imagery so that by the time I eventually would step into the Congo I already knew what it was going to feel like. Still, to this day I'll never forget that night in the ministry; a light snow fell, and the lights of the library and a classroom building filled our space. Our shoes and socks sat soaked on vents with warm air blowing, and we found some red wine in the kitchen cabinet and poured two glasses. Then he talked about starting in the south, near Lubumbashi, and crossing the equator two times. By the time we put on our dry socks we had been standing on Banana Beach, celebrating. It was as if we planned the trip, went, returned, and sat and reminisced all in the span of a few hours. It was a good night, talking like most people talk who never get to go but let their minds wander sometimes. Some journeys are at their best then, and there is no need to go anywhere. Some adventures reach their peak during this stage, almost satisfied to burn out before beginning. Unfortunately, that wasn't the case this time.

Before we returned to the dorm, he sat quietly again for a while, then said, "You know, it seems a lot scarier from here than once you're there and you see kids with their mothers walking around a village, or you walk into cities with buses and street vendors. When you know the languages, you really don't care all that much about any possible 'dangers' any more than you would heading up to Buffalo on a Saturday night."

"I suppose," I said, but added with some hesitation. "But, honestly Joe, we don't have the equivalent of the deep Congo River region, remote villages, mercenaries, untreatable diseases. There's no Urgent Care in the Congo. No convenience stores. Our trip—your trip—is in one of the most remote, least understood places on the planet. You're not hanging out in Rochester for a weekend."

"No! That would be more dangerous!" We laughed; a bit carelessly, perhaps.

The wilderness, though, is where he and I could relate; it was our common ground. I grew up feeling much more comfortable in the woods and wetlands of eastern Long Island and coastal Virginia than in the streets of New York City, or even Buffalo. I told him this so he knew I could relate, but added, "Of course, I never saw a croc on the

Island. Or a snake for that matter. I grew up in wooded suburbia."

"No hippos, either?"

"Hardly any," I said, and we walked to get breakfast. Now, all these years later I understand all of our laughter was simply a relief of our anxiety, some sort of defense mechanism. For thirty-five years I've stood victim to the ridicule and curses of nineteen-year-olds. I've had desks thrown at me, threats, abusive comments, and threatening notes handed to me. Yet in nearly all cases, their inexcusable actions have been mostly the result of nervousness, fear, sometimes the terror of failing and dealing with an abusive parent. It took years for me to understand the difference between a passing, humorous comment and one borne of anxiety. It was the same for me back then. Still, that night in the ministry remains with more clarity than perhaps any other time for me at the college. We did the entire journey that night, talked it through. And I pull that night out once in a while and paddle up the reaches of my memory from time to time. No translation is necessary. For a brief time one night there were no language barriers, no waterfalls or province invasions, no intestinal diseases, little weakness or succumbing. There was just a couple of young men making plans, ignoring the one obvious problem we could not train for: No one had ever done this alone.

What it came down to is the complete absence of any common ground between life in the States, especially in rural New York State, and life along the Congo River. It is more than just language, which might be the primary barrier if one were to canoe the Seine River. Everything is measured differently in Africa. I was beginning to wonder if we were in over our heads.

Six

Alone

Another drastic contrast between the planning of the trip which we did surrounded by friends and faculty, to the reality of canoeing the Congo alone for what might be six or seven months, was that gap between companionship and isolation. Two psychology professors who taught Joe while he was a psychology major assisted us in figuring out how to temper the shock of extreme loneliness.

"Write letters, keep a journal, basic communication, albeit without immediate response, will keep the ghosts of loneliness at bay," one of the professors suggested. Cole chimed in every chance he could with suggestions like, "Find a girl to go!" or "Canoe the Mississippi and I'll visit you! Hell, even Kunzinger can find the Mississippi!" Sometimes Cole carried comic relief too far into the artery of what was about to happen. But we both agreed that his humor was the only way we could address the element of things unknown. It helped temper the one aspect of the trip you cannot plan for. It sounds obvious, of course, that one cannot anticipate what they do not know, let alone understand, but in the mix of measuring a journey of the most dangerous proportions—a truth of this journey I did not comprehend for decades after my own journey there—it is easy to simply push aside that which you know you will never grasp to begin with, relegate it to the shoreline as misguided energy, instead of pushing on, working it until some answer reveals itself. And the truth is it was as easy then as it is now to write off psychological issues as secondary at best, tertiary more likely, to the primary concerns of trying not to be killed by animals or bacteria. And that way of thinking seemed fair enough. When Joe arrived at the Atlantic, if the worst thing that happened is he complained about how lonely he was out there, we'd consider it quite the success indeed.

We did not understand, nor do I recall the professors exploring the residual effects of loneliness on the body, on lethargy, on apathy and a loss of attention to vital details, which likely would keep Joe alive. And if any of that seemed out of the realm of possibility in Allegany, New York, we couldn't possibly comprehend what would slide in his trajectory while out on The Congo.

"I have trained for loneliness," Joe told me one morning. "Most of my time in the village was spent alone; and riding my bike all those times all that distance was a lonely experience."

"That's different," I said. "In both cases you could have talked to anyone at any time. Hell, on the bike you could have pulled into a 711 and chatted away the afternoon. In the village you were surrounded by others, including an American PC worker who was not far away most of the time."

Being alone and loneliness are not the same thing, I told him like I knew what I was talking about. I thought of my bike days that first summer in the south. "I don't think it is an issue for me anymore than it would be an issue for a sailor circumnavigating the globe, like that kid you talked about." Robin Lee Graham. "It's there, yes, but there are more important issues that make loneliness a small concern."

I agreed.

Joe and I both discovered that in centuries past no one publicly entertained the notion of traveling alone. Henry Stanley often had hundreds of people to help him. At the library one evening, Joe flipped through a bio of Stanley's life and noted he had attempted the same trip exactly one hundred years earlier. That increased Joe's motivation. "Exactly one hundred years!" he exclaimed. The anniversary didn't drive him; the fact no one could accomplish this simple feat despite journeys to other remote places on the planet, including the poles, intrigued Joe. "It's time," he said, and tipped back his round leather hat. In rare moments when he wasn't sure of himself, I noticed how he would finger the piece of ivory always dangling from his neck. During that year, Joe rarely touched it. Once, when I asked about animals, he ran his hand from his coat pocket to his neck, sliding his fingers down the silver chain to the malachite capped tip of the ivory tooth.

"You see," he said, "That's the only part we can't possibly predict; no one can control where those things will go," he said, laughing. He meant hippos, crocs, snakes. "Sleeping inside a metal box is the only foolproof way to avoid them," he'd joke. "Of course, knowing how they act during dry and rainy seasons helps, it really does."

The trip would have to start in autumn because of the rain. He'd cross the equator twice and finish in late spring, April, maybe May. "Gotta watch the rain," became our mantra. The region enjoys generally high temperatures and is under the influence of both the Indian and Atlantic Oceans. The north is an equatorial zone, whereas the east is a mountainous region. Therefore, the Congo River is characterized by two annual swellings: A big swelling in December thanks to the rainy season in the Southern Hemisphere, and a second flooding in May because of the rainy season in the Northern Hemisphere. As a consequence, there are also two dry seasons, the worst in August.

For Henry Stanley, who had to deal with the diseases and conditions of one hundred years earlier, the rainy seasons were equally important. In 1881, Stanley, having already mapped the Congo River from just past present-day Kisangani west to Banana on the Atlantic, attempted to complete the task by traveling from the source of the Congo near Lumbumbashi up across the equator. Several years earlier, Stanley had become a legend when the *New York Herald* sent the young reporter to Africa to find the lost missionary, David Livingstone.

During Stanley's second Congo River expedition from its source, many of his men died from diseases such as malaria brought on by the rains. Others abandoned him. The longer he remained in Africa, the less likely it seemed he would ever leave alive. Like Livingstone, of whom Joseph Conrad wrote, "Passion had changed him in his last days from a great explorer into a restless wanderer refusing to go home anymore," Stanley's own passion for Africa overshadowed his mission to map the continent. He first went to Africa reluctantly, his sole purpose to search for and bring home Livingstone. When he found him, Stanley discovered the missionary-explorer had befriended the Africans and learned their customs. The two became close friends, "father and son," as he wrote. He joined Livingstone on travels where the two sought the Nile's source, but he left before they had accomplished the feat. After Livingstone died, Stanley returned to complete his mentor's projects.

Stanley's critics said he fabricated stories about Livingstone, despite proof in Livingstone's journals. One dissenter in the Royal Geographic Society at the time insisted that no one support Stanley. "His enthusiasm has shrouded his purpose," he wrote. "He will fail." He didn't, fueled by his love of both Livingstone and Africa.

We worked in the Friedsam Memorial Library and noted significant differences to emerge in the century between Stanley and Kohn. Joe had medicine for the diseases, maps of the tributaries as well as the Congo (maps, ironically, first documented by Stanley), and a priceless personal knowledge of the people and their customs. In those one hundred years, however, the river had not become less dangerous—every bend in the river hid possible troubles from animal attacks to warring villagers—but the river had become less mysterious.

Not long ago I wondered what would happen if he made the trip today? He would have his cellphone and laptop, probably a website so others could track his progress, a medical team in a different canoe, and perhaps even a small boat to sleep in instead of risking his life on shore or in the canoe. He'd have GPS navigation and depth finders. None of this, I think I can accurately say, would interest Joe at all.

Joe and I studied those maps of the Congo lit by dim desk lamps on century-old tables. Within a few months, we knew the topography, the horticulture, the language, and the cultures. We knew the average annual rainfall was over eighty inches; we knew that the temperature in January kept close to seventy and in July ninety. We memorized elevations on different sections of the river, ranging from sixteen hundred feet to around five thousand. The history and social science departments taught us of President Mobutu and his dictatorship, and of the United States' support of Zaire during the troubles with Angola. We learned Mobutu tried to live up to his name, Mobutu Sese Seko Kuku Ngbendu wa za Banga, which means "The all-powerful warrior who, because of his inflexible will to win, will go from conquest to conquest leaving fire in his wake." We studied the Carter administration's objections to Mobutu's human rights records. With the trip coming just after Reagan took office, Zaire's interest in the United States would be strong again. Every little bit helped. We studied with noted interest the Shaba invasions from Angola into Zaire's Shaba Province two years earlier. For one, the two rebel invasions had just happened, and two, the tricky parts of Joe's journey were located in the Shaba Province. We mapped the course through the eastern portion of the Shaba Province, so we studied its politics. We digested mathematical skills for navigation. We ate sun-dried fish. We talked.

Seven

Mountains of the Moon

When we opened maps and reference books of the region, talk turned to river travel, missionaries, and mercenaries, so eventually students pulled chairs closer. Whispers gained volume while even librarians gathered and listened.

Joe liked the audience. I don't ever remember a time in the library when Joe and I were not surrounded by students and librarians. The only difference between the Friedsam Library and Antonio's was three hundred yards and a plate of chicken wings.

The plan was for Joe to complete the journey in the spring. When he crossed the equator a second time on the downhill slide to Banana Beach, the trip would be just about finished. The entire region toward the end of the trip was densely populated, unlike the remote, nearly undiscovered territory in the Southeast and South where the Lualaba River meets the Congo and bleeds north from the Shaba Province. Down there, difficult navigation and even minor mishaps can escalate to life and death episodes. That's why we waded through river maps and reference materials: to minimize the risk. This was three decades before GPS mapping.

"I won't die, Bob, really," he said once on our way

back from Letchworth State Park where we had camped one weekend. I believed him, of course. I was nineteen. We diligently prepared for death, its methods and motivations. Every problem united automatically with a solution. Many months of preparation provided the pretense that nothing was left about which to concern ourselves. *Off Course*: Find villagers for guides and directions, follow the stars, use the compass. *Sick*: Rest and follow the plan outlined on dysentery, influenza, malaria, seek refuge and boil water at a village. *Attacked by rebels*: Steer away from known trouble areas, like near Angola in the Shaba province; and don't carry guns or large knives; use cameras as protection by promising to convey the group's cause to the world, carry the *National Geographic* letter which suggests their interest in his story. We knew how one could die in the Congo and how to avoid death. "I've had dysentery more than a few times," he told me. I would challenge him; remind him that when he had such ailments, he was in a village, but he always shook it off. "Do we have medicine for that?" It was rhetorical, of course. It was almost always rhetorical.

This was the most adult thing I'd ever done, and while I was just nineteen, we took this seriously. This was not two guys who came up with a plan during some wild drunken stupor. This was precise work entailing deep planning and constant double-checking of all information. My professor of Research Methods, George Evans, was indispensable in suggesting sources which could not be refuted and which, when the information contradicted other sources, could be shown to be more accurate.

Mostly, we concerned ourselves with the most likely ailments. When Joe lived in eastern Zaire in 1979, epidemic dysentery swept the region. At its mildest form, epidemic dysentery produces diarrhea with blood. From there, bowels deteriorate, and seizures follow. Renal failure is right behind with a mortality rate of about fifteen percent. Contaminated water and food cause its transmission in impoverished areas. Antibiotics help but are not available upon demand a thousand miles from Kinshasa.

I thought about this as we waded in Lake Chautauqua. On the south bank, tall, thick pines bent over the water like a canopy, their roots exposed from erosion. And back on the Allegheny River we walked across rocks in the middle while cool, shallow water ran west past our ankles. It was September and the sun warmed my back. I stared at the river as if it were the Congo. Nearby, villagers might have been bathing, cleaning clothes, fishing, urinating, defecating, throwing garbage in the river. Here, in New York, a few students walked a nearby trail. One of them, eating a sandwich, waved. The memory of that student's wave, so casual and friendly and safe, haunts me. What naivete I carried at nineteen to believe the Congo and the Allegheny had anything in common. But back then, back there, we knew what we were doing, of course. We had it all under control. Of course we did. And there was no difference between the two rivers; even Joe played off of Gertrude Stein's famous rose by exclaiming more than a few times, that "a river is a river is a river."

No. It's not. I may have received a C- in Middle Eastern Geography and History from Fr. Bob White during which we also talked about Africa a bit, but I understood every aspect of the far reaches of the Congo River, and I didn't even receive credit.

Here's what I learned:

The Zairean landscape is as diverse as the Congo River is long. In the east a low-lying river basin rises to a forested plateau, eventually climbing nearly 17,000 feet to the summit of Mt. Stanley in the Ruwenzori Mountains, the so-called "Mountains of the Moon." Along the country's eastern edge, a chain of lakes links the Great Rift Valley, including Albert, Edward, Kivu, and Tanganyika. The west coast, however, has just twenty-seven miles of Atlantic coast.

The Congo runs through all of present-day Democratic Republic of Congo. Formed by a junction of the Lualaba and Luvua Rivers in the south, the Congo flows north as far as Stanley Falls, then loops west and south to an outlet on the South Atlantic Ocean at Banana Beach. The river is sixteen kilometers wide at times, about ten miles, and contains more than four thousand islands. The Congo basin includes most of the Republic of Congo, northern Angola, northern Zambia, western Tanzania, and the southern Central African Republic. It is densely covered with tropical vegetation, particularly in the river valleys. And the wildlife includes crocodiles, hippos, and countless species of fish.

The Congo is the country's transportation and economic aorta, divided in four sections: The Headwaters, the Upper Congo, the Middle Congo, and the Lower Congo. The river's most remote headstreams rise in northern Zambia and southern Congo, in elevations ranging from three thousand to seven thousand feet above sea level. Rapids break these waters often, and so they cannot be used for commercial navigation, and even small boats—rafts—can reach dangerous currents and falls along the route. Back in Zambia, The Chambeshi and other streams drain into Lake Bangweulu, a shallow lake surrounded by swamps. That lake overflows into the Luapula, the border between Zambia and Zaire, where the Congo flows into Lake Mweru.

Not much further.

Lake Mweru drains into the Luvua in Zaire. In the southern Congo, the Lualaba and its headwaters rise in the highlands of the Katanga region. The Lualaba is joined by the Lufira at Lake Upemba and flows north to meet the Luvua in northern Katanga.

The Upper Congo, which is often thought of as a continuation of the Lualaba, flows north toward Stanley Falls, also called Boyoma Falls. But only one stretch of about two hundred miles is navigable. Beyond Ubundu, a chain of seven cataracts makes the river impassable for about sixty miles, unless one travels by canoe or raft, but all the locals say that is too dangerous because of wildlife in the region which thrives where ships can't pass. Stanley Falls, the last of the cataracts, is thirty miles north of the equator. Kisangani, one of the largest cities in the country, lies just below the falls.

I looked up from the maps at the table in the main hall of the library, then looked around to make sure no one was within earshot. "Why would you do this ?" I whispered. We had been talking with others, but they had either left or returned to a nearby table to do their own work. Joe sometimes interrupted me to correct my pronunciation of the villages or river names, or to tell a brief story about the area; usually a humorous story giving everyone the impression this is just a trip down the Allegheny to Salamanca, and we'll all have some beef on weck sandwiches in no time.

"Seriously, why are you doing this?"

He looked at me, then back at the map, pointing to the next region. "Go on," he said. He never didn't smile. The entire stretch of the Middle Congo is navigable as it curves northwest then west then southwest. The four rivers, the Lomami, the Aruwimi, the Ubangi, and the Kasai rivers are the primary tributaries. The Ubangi is the largest tributary of the Congo and flows down from the border with the Central African Republic. About one hundred miles below the mouth of another river, the Kwa, the Congo widens to form a lake, called Pool Malabo. When the river narrows again, the capitals of the Congo and the Republic of the Congo face each other from opposite banks of the river—Kinshasa, Zaire, on the south bank, and Brazzaville, Republic of Congo, on the north.

"Then I'll get word to you to get on a plane. Mel will meet you in Kinshasa and drive you out to Banana. I know a place." I laughed, and the positive energy pushed my question off the table.

The Lower Congo from Pool Malabo to the Atlantic is just two hundred and seventy miles long. Wild rapids make most of this stretch unnavigable to all but small river craft. The last of the rapids is ninety-five miles from the sea. The port of Matadi is on the south bank. A railroad connects Kinshasa and Matadi. Next is the border between Congo and Angola before emptying into the Atlantic at Banana Beach.

"If we time it right and I can get near Kinshasa after you're done with the semester, then you'll be able to meet me there as I pass, hang out in the city for a few days, then head out with Mel to celebrate the completion!" My thin nineteen-year-old mind sat contemplating spending a month or so in Kinshasa after my freshman year in college. Whether or not this was a good idea was irrelevant. My mind immediately considered that I'd have to learn more French, get a new camera, and save my money for the trip. Joe suggested using some of the money from selling the stones for my airfare.

The world in 1980 was desperately out of sorts. The Iranian hostage crisis was underway where fifty-two Americans had been held for four hundred and forty-four days, and the nightly news had been occupied with updates on that. The 1980 election between Carter and Reagan was underway, and how that went would determine how relations might go in Zaire. Even getting in and out of the country could be tricky depending upon Mobutu's frame of mind about the election results. The trip would be more than halfway over by the time the new president would take or retain office, but in countries as unstable as those in central Africa at the time, it was difficult to tell how even the primaries might affect the mood.

Still, I knew more about Africa than the Middle East, much to the disappointment of Fr. Bob. He pointed out more than a few times how in class I was either asleep or deep in thought with my head in my own notes about Africa instead of his notes about Middle Eastern History. "I know what you and Mr. Kohn are doing," he said once, "and it is admirable if not just a little careless." Fr. always could speak to you in a stern yet fatherly way instead of sounding like a pissed-off professor. "But you spend too much of your time in class lost in the Congo. You need to pay more attention to your schoolwork, Mr. Kunzinger. Has anyone ever told you that?" he asked.

Everyone, I thought. "No, Father."

Eight

The Explorers

"Why are you doing this?" I asked again. Sometimes I'd ask in a joking way, like two guys about to skydive for the first time. Other times, I'd be more serious, perhaps phrase it in a different way. That was how I asked this time. We were on the trail near the river.

"I don't know," he said. In a rare moment of self-analysis, he stopped walking and looked around. "Maybe I'm trying to find myself." We laughed and continued the research, anticipated the problems, engaged in role-playing scenarios to ready him for too much rain, too little food, linguistic jeopardy. We even marked what we called "safe areas" for him to go while in-country—a lake in the northeast, a village in the east—if he felt in danger and needed to wait out a storm, literally or metaphorically, or sweat away some illness. Still, I pushed him more than a few times on the question of why and he never came up with the same answer, or a satisfying one, for him or for me. "It just makes sense to me, Bob." Then he laughed, moved on, and I was never sure if he simply remained light-hearted about everything or if he truly couldn't explain it. Years later when discussing careers and "the future" with my students about how to choose a major or a career, that phrase kept creeping back into my lectures; "It just has to make sense to you, even if you can't explain it to anyone else." And I meant it, believed it, albeit forty years too late.

"Have you ever heard of Carl Akeley?"

I thought for a minute. "Yes, but I don't know why. I've seen his name a lot in our explorer notes."

"You might have studied his work in Cole's art history class."

"He's an artist?"

"A sculptor."

"So what about Carl Akeley?"

"He died of fever and is buried on Mt Mikeno in central Africa."

Joe had my attention, so I returned to the stack of explorer books and looked him up. Akeley, a taxidermist, hailed from western New York as did Joe, but his desire was to explore the Congo's beauty, understand its citizens, and preserve its natural wonders. He died there in 1926. First, however, Akeley invented the cement guns used to line the Panama Canal, conceived of the first rotary motion picture camera, and developed a search light for the military. He survived a mauling by a bull elephant, according to several accounts killed a leopard with his hands, and he hunted with Teddy Roosevelt. His sculptures remain in museums throughout the world, and he established Africa's first game reserve, Parc National Albert, with the aid of the Belgian government in 1925. He fell in love with the gorillas of the eastern Congo, a few of which still wander the Virunga Mountains, hiding from poachers and rebels.

"Stop thinking of this place as unexplored territory, Bob. I'm not the first. I'm not even the first from western New York!" I never missed the opportunity to mention this to those who suggested this was a fool's errand, and there were plenty of fools like us before we came along.

"I'm not, really. In fact, I'm thinking of lots of explorers who have been there. You know, the ones that never returned, like Carl here."

"Ingredients," he would always reply. "They didn't have all the ingredients."

Joe spent as much time in the region as any of the previous explorers in history. He spoke more languages than any previous intruder. He had more protection against and knowledge of diseases than absolutely any other adventurer to enter The Congo. For credentials, Joe's swamped the competition in every aspect.

"Tell me about the beginning."

The Congo's source is narrow, its long veins of dark, murky water spilling through brush and marsh. One must, if he wishes to start here, hack his way through with a machete south of Lumbumbashi, sometimes hauling the boat and supplies around trails, often through villages where no one assists but everyone watches. The arteries widen quickly, and about one thousand miles south of Kisangani, the Congo River begins in earnest. Henry Stanley wrote of the region in *The Founding of the Congo Free State*, in 1885: "Beyond the village was low forested land, which either came in dense black towering masses of impenetrable vegetation to the waterside, or else ran in great semicircles half enclosing grassy flats, whereon hippopotami fed at nighttime."

What happens on the river after that is anybody's guess, and many died guessing. Dying is not new to Africa, and certainly not to The Congo.

In 1346, Jaime Ferrer disappeared exploring West Africa. He had hoped to establish trade routes, something

Antonio Gonsalves would do one hundred years later, when he also introduced African slaves to Portugal. Nunno Tristaao died from poison arrows on his way back from the Gambia in 1447 after he attempted to enslave them, hoping to follow Gonsalves up the economic ladder created by slavery. Daniel Houghton had Moor guides through West Africa who subsequently robbed him and left him to battle his wounds and starvation. He lost. Henry Nichols explored Guinea in1805 and died there of fever. Not malaria but a simple flu which a few cups of tea might have cornered and killed. A year later, Mungo Park drowned in Nigeria fleeing locals. His journey was not for money and slavery; he simply wished to map the territory. Walter Oudney succumbed to illness in Senegal in 1824. Hugh Clapperton met the same fate in Nigeria in 1827.

Johann Burckhardt in 1817, Friedrich Hornemann in 1801, David Livingstone in 1873 all surrendered to dysentery. Alexander Laing's guide murdered him in 1826 near Timbuktu, though it isn't certain why. James Richardson died from malaria around 1852. Officials in the Free Congo State ordered Eduard Vogel assassinated in 1865, accused of spying. In 1869, near Ghat, Libya, roving Tuaregs killed explorer Alexandrine Tinnee. In 1916, nearby in Algeria, radical Muslims killed Charles-Eugene de Foucauld. Meanwhile, Eduard Schnitzer was beheaded by Arab soldiers on orders of a local chief.

From the first recorded visit by a European, Portuguese navigator Diogo Cam, in 1482, the Congo River, the source of life for its people, has been the source of death for its visitors. Originally, the river was called the Zaire, a variation of a local term, Mzadi, meaning "great water." Explorers later referred to it as the Congo for the Kongo kingdom located near the mouth of the river. Its official name flowed and ebbed between Zaire and Congo for forty years, though it will always be referred to primarily as The Congo.

Europe had a field day with The Congo. While the earliest native inhabitants of the region were Pygmies, Bantu peoples displaced most of them when they came to mine copper in the south around 700 A.D. Today, the Pygmy population has dwindled to less than eight thousand. When Cam traveled to the Congo from Portugal, Europe showed interest, but it wasn't until the Berlin conference of 1884-85 that colonization took hold. At the time of the conference, about eighty percent of Africa remained under local and traditional rule. The original purpose of the conference was to guarantee the Congo and Niger River mouths and basins would remain neutral and open to trade. The United States, European nations, and the Ottoman Empire intended to adjust territorial control of the African colonies. Instead, European powers had superimposed boundaries separating about fifty nations over nearly one thousand indigenous cultures and regions of the continent. King Leopold of Belgium controlled the lands surrounding the Congo River, but mapping and exploration became necessities for trade and control. Until the eighteenth century, European control of Africa remained solely along coastal regions, but exploration by Henry Stanley for King Leopold unearthed not just maps but resources in Africa's interior.

Other Europeans tried to demystify Africa, namely Sir Richard Burton, John Hanning Speke and David Livingstone. Burton and Speke spent years exploring eastern and central Africa. At first their "safaris," a phrase Burton coined, centered on locating the source of the Nile River, but they failed. Still, in doing so, the two discovered Lake Tanganyika and had to deal with Egyptian caravans. Speke left Burton and continued, but he wasn't so good at it solo. His accounts of the region are laced with fallacies, generalizations, and miscalculations, but his timeless descriptions in daily logs maintain a view of the region not many journals have recorded. Still, he remains historically a second-rate explorer. He discovered Lake Victoria, but in 1864 shot himself. It could have been disappointment at his lack of world fame while his former partner, Burton, continued in legendary fashion. Or it could have been illness, malaria perhaps. Loneliness cannot be ruled out, either.

David Livingstone became famous for disappearing, or, more precisely, seeming to disappear. In fact, while England considered him dead, he remained a missionary, explorer, and recorder of village activity in eastern and central Africa, noting the people's patience and practicality, marking customs with admiration and respect. He lived among the people, remarking, however, that Europeans truly were not only more cultivated, but of a superior class. This racism, however, did not compromise his friendship with Africans. One infamous experience occurred when he watched slave traders slaughter villagers, and it became his mission to get that story told, to expose the British slavery which still existed, and in doing so, end it. He died before that happened, but Stanley carried Livingstone's journals containing those notes back to England where they were promptly published. Livingstone relied on Africans for travel, communication, and company. He learned their language, discovered their ways and adopted their customs in exchange for an occasional sermon. In 1871 he stumbled upon the Lualaba River while searching for the source of the Nile. It was while he was "missing" in Ujiji that New York Herald reporter Henry Morton Stanley walked into town, followed by a hundred or so Africans hired to assist him. His famous greeting, "Dr. Livingstone, I presume?"

remains a symbol of lost and found, of hope at the end of hopelessness. When Livingstone died of dysentery in 1873, his African friends carried him to the coast for transport home where he was buried in Westminster Cathedral. His ideas and plans, however, remained scattered about Africa, and Stanley returned to continue the search for the Nile's source. In doing so, the Anglo-American, whose real name was John Rowlands, introduced the Belgians, who financed his journeys, to the Congo. In the thirty years before he died in 1904, Stanley traveled and mapped the Congo, carrying with him enough native people to fill several villages. In 1877 he mapped eight hundred miles south of Kisangani to the Iruri River, moving closer to the source of the Congo. When fifty-two of his men could not continue, Stanley, crippled by leg ulcers, malaria, and malnutrition, left them in what became known as "starvation camp." They all died.

In 1885, in Berlin, Stanley played an instrumental part in the division of Africa. Leopold II of Belgium, thanks in large part to Stanley's documents, secured the Congo despite claims made by the French. Both countries employed their claimed villagers to wage war against each other, speaking new languages and practicing new religions. What Livingstone tried to preserve, Stanley attempted to homogenize into Belgian customs. In fact, in his journals he shows his enthusiasm for Belgium's control of the Congo. He wrote "The romance of the wild land is all gone. Instead we have something approaching order and system and peaceful intercourse. Success has amply crowned my efforts. Thanks and praise be to God! May he nourish it to mature fullness to be a shining example to the rest of that continent, which remained so long dark and mysterious."

The African pie now lay cut up into various European slices of French, Belgian, English, Portuguese, and Dutch.

Even the Germans did what they could when explorer Emin Pasha, whose real name was Dr. Edouard Schnitzer, traveled with Stanley to Mombasa. In 1885 warring factions cut him off from the expedition during the Mahdist uprising, and in 1892 villagers beheaded him near Lake Tanganyika. Stanley marched on, writing books and lecturing throughout Europe and the United States about the colonization of Africa and the Congo. Intrigued by his writings and explorations, Polish born writer and seaman Joseph Conrad decided to see for himself what existed beyond the mouth of the Congo River at Banana Beach on the Atlantic. In 1890, he traveled upriver, recording in his journals what would later become *Heart of Darkness*. The "darkness" he surveyed, despite his obvious racist attitude, was the European approach to the carnage it imposed upon a natural and pure territory. It was Conrad who followed Stanley in his attempts to expose and eradicate British domination over central Africa. Certainly, Conrad was no saint; he didn't have Livingstone's integrity or the guilt which plagued Speke. In fact, Conrad's racism painted a gory picture of central Africa which lasted well into the twentieth century. That attitude, however, precedes Conrad's work and falls squarely on the shoulders of King Leopold and his Belgian representatives. The classic epigraph to mark the beginning of control and domination by the Europeans, and, in turn, the hatred of villagers throughout the Congo region toward "English," no matter their origin, comes from the Belgian Premier, M. de Smet de Naeyer, representing King Leopold. He wrote, "The native is entitled to nothing. What is given to him is a pure gratuity." As a result, explorers who wished merely to observe instead of conquer, map instead of claim, came upon local people who had no interest in assisting any more "English."

***

This history, preceding Joe's trip by a century, remained relevant. On our maps we marked the villages where Joe might find food. He pointed to some villages and explained languages they probably spoke, which ones they despised. Some villages have a history of enslavement by Europeans, others can easily recall "English" taking lands for mining or claiming markets for trade. Joe wanted to avoid these. He traced for me the rebellions in the Shaba province and where the rebels most likely remained. None of this sounded dangerous, just cautionary. Those involved in the territory had their own agenda, whether it be political or economic, and Joe didn't factor into anybody's plan. "Danger from animals existed when he lived in Africa, so why would he suddenly forget his training and knowledge?" remained our response to anyone who protested Joe's ignorance of Africa's wildlife. The river, to us, seemed simply a highway, that's all. Along the road were possible rockslides, potholes, crazy drivers and very few rest stops. We consulted the equivalent of every travel agency available and digested advice. We considered weather patterns, rebel fronts, disease, food supplies, sleeplessness, and starvation. We knew the price better than Stanley knew his, or Livingstone, or most of the others.

One hundred years earlier, Joe's predecessors didn't travel alone: the adventurers remained in groups, as did Stanley, Livingstone, and Burton. To divert from this already trodden path, twentieth century travelers had to step up to another level. Had Joe joined any of the campaigns one hundred years earlier, today he might be considered part of history, recorded on the finest pages of the Royal Geographic Society, and villages along the Congo would carry his name: Kohnville, Joseph Falls. Instead, timing teased his ambition to seek more, to go solo.

We sat at Antonio's for the last time, this time alone.

"You ever wonder why the Congo *hasn't* been done entirely by one person?" I asked. I expected his usual quip, "Ingredients!" but instead, he thought for a moment while eating another chicken wing.

He wiped his hands and sat back. "You have to have the right background. I have the combination of experiences needed, and now with the studying we've done, I've filled in the rest of the blank spaces. And maybe most people who would even consider such a trip think of it too simplistically." The truth is, it was only Joe who made it seem that simple.

We knew that once Joe made it past Kabalo and Kisangani, we could practically celebrate. I would fly to Kinshasa and head to Banana Beach with whatever press I could muster. *National Geographic* would not commit financially but agreed to see what happened. *The Voice of America* thrived on material like this, and of course the American newspapers already aware of his trip were eager for a successful completion. We knew the languages, the social boundaries, we knew which villages were where and when to stop and when to keep paddling, we knew when he could rest and when he had to cross the equator the first time, we knew the rain patterns and the migratory patterns, we knew what supplies were still needed and which ones he could abandon if he had to, we made copies of the maps for small waterproof pouches, and we put the originals in my room for me to take home, we were so ready.

Nine

Once

"What if you get lost?" I asked. I knew immediately I had asked an adolescent question. He had lived in the Congo for nearly four years. He knew the languages, the people, the customs, and culture; he knew their spin on life. "The people in the region will get me through," he said. "I've traveled there before when living in the village. Really, I'll be fine," he said, smiling. And that was it. In all of our hundreds of hours of research, of trekking through rivers and reservoirs, of studying previous explorers and writers and of all the psychologists we talked to, that evening for those thirty seconds was the only time we spent contemplating Joe getting lost.

Something else occurred to me much later; he was twenty-seven years old. At nineteen, those years between us were enough to make him seem like a guru, an elder statesman who had been where I stood and made it to where I decided I wanted to go. Twenty-seven is ancient to a nineteen-year-old. That's a third of my life older than me. So from my perspective he had the answers and had been around the block enough times to know what he was talking about. Now, after staring at nineteen-year-olds for thirty-five years, as well as teaching retiring military in their forties and fifties, I understand that twenty-seven-years old is innocent, naive. He was a kid, and in retrospect it isn't difficult to see we were both in way over our heads. But his confidence bled into mine, and when he did have a rare moment of doubt, I found it my job to boost him back up, remind him of the traits he possessed that will make the trip successful. By the time he left I was absolutely certain I could do this entire journey myself, and I had never even been to Africa.

Ten

Departure

It was time to leave. The previous morning Joe had dropped his sister off at kindergarten, took his trunk of supplies and boarded a bus to Olean, and came to campus. The previous night we had walked to Antonio's and sat in the lounge, then this morning he woke on the floor to the sound of his watch alarm he picked up in Rio.

"What classes do you have today?" he asked.

"Media Law," I said, suddenly once again inexplicably completely disinterested in the very notion of being a college student. In some odd way I felt like the learning was over and it was graduation day.

Joe and I sat on the bottom steps in the dormitory stairwell and waited for the taxi to take him to the Bluebird Bus Station in Olean for the ride to New York City for his flight through Brussels to Kinshasa. It was raining. "I wish I were your age and did the things I did," he said. He was twenty-seven.

I laughed. "I hope in my entire life that I've done half the things you've done," I said. He smiled, and we looked under grey skies toward the hills behind campus, toward Merton's Heart—that clearing in the woods where what seemed liked so long ago we laughed and planned and anticipated. The

Allegheny River ran beneath the morning mist, and no one was about. There had never been this much silence between us. He fingered the ivory tooth about his neck.

"My dad thinks I should accept the graduate thing at Cornell. I was getting in the car to drop my sister off before I headed down here, and the last thing he said to me was, 'When are you ever going to settle down?'" Joe had applied to veterinary school. This melancholy was unprecedented. He wore a flowered shirt from Zaire and his leather hat. I think we both would rather have been laughing at Antonio's. I searched the sky for some signs of clearing. A door slammed, and a few students staggered by heading toward breakfast, smelling of beer. They were just another sign of my early days at college when I felt like I would never fit in; those days surrounded by drunken stupors and crass comments seemed ancient history, a younger version of myself whose skin I had finally shed. I fit in fine now by the most remarkable of circumstances; by not caring whether I fit in or not.

We sat in the stairwell a long time.

"Don't forget to call Mel in Kinshasa when you get the plane ticket. He'll pick you up at the airport to meet me on the coast."

"I've got it memorized," I said, which was true. Every aspect of the trip was clear to me, as if it was spread out like maps on library tables before me. I breathed The Congo, could taste its murky waters. I could not wait for Spring. I planned for and anticipated this trip for almost a year; now I just wanted it to be over. All trips are different for those of us left behind—slower, vague, more dangerous.

When the taxi arrived, we managed to get his trunk in the back seat. The magnitude of this venture had not yet settled in for me. In fact, as I stood in the courtyard of my college dorm, I finally recognized how incomprehensible it all really was. For me, on the one hand, just the planning itself had been the adventure; on the other, I felt to my soul I should be making the trip with him, that somehow for some reason I really needed to go. Despite the reality of the word "solo" having hung over this journey from the start, I spent the previous months planning as if this was an African version of Lewis and Clark. In my mind I was going, and it was that simple.

"Get me a shirt like that, would you?" I asked.

"Sure," he said. "And you contact the State Department and get me some maps of the Amazon." He smiled again. This was his trademark, planning ahead. Adventurers do not discuss trips, really. They plan them and take them. The Congo trip, after all, was simply practice.

Under stormy skies we shook hands, embraced, and he left. As the taxi pulled away, he rolled down the window and called out to me. "This is our trip!" I believed that, despite his departure and my sudden return to stagnancy. Still, at the time I could not possibly know it would quite literally become my trip.

I stood in the courtyard until the car rolled to the main highway and drove off. Class started in thirty minutes, but I had no desire to go. After what had been almost a year during which I was driven to excel in my courses, understand whatever I could, I had almost instantly become indifferent again. Some switch in my mind seemed to have shut off, forcing me to return to an apathetic state. A week earlier all course content seemed relevant, essential to some grander purpose. But as the taxi disappeared and students came and went, classes flowed back into some mundane current. I walked around the dorm and saw the taxi at the stop sign, and Joe waved through the back window, and he was gone.

Eleven

Letters

These excerpts are from Joe's letters to various people, though most are to me.

1.
The beginning was really tough. The river is so narrow in parts that the trees fall completely across. I had to hack my way through with a machete and pull my boat through at times. I only covered a few miles a day at first. I went over a small waterfall and broke open my waterproof pouches. Everything got wet and ruined my camera and film. I have more and another waiting in Kinshasa. I'm going to have it sent out. I hope it gets here before I leave again.

2.
After all my matches got wet and I had to survive by eating raw fish dried in the sun, I thought of you! I didn't carry enough food supplies to last me. We figured I could get to Kolwezi in a couple of days, but the river is slow at the beginning and there were no people to get supplies from. All those others marked on our maps no longer exist, either from flooda times or it being a warring zone now.

Things here changed a lot in the couple of years since I was here last.

3.

Get the presses rolling! Contact the Buffalo and New York papers and that guy who wrote from National Geographic! *What would really get the ball rolling is contact the* Voice of America *in Washington. This is really important. They thrive on stuff like this. I am sure they will broadcast it. Also great would be to contact the* Armed Forces Radio and Television Service. *See who Jandoli can contact. Get all the promotions going. I am going to make it. I've gotten through the hardest part. I'll probably be done in ten more weeks. My boat is in terrible shape, but I've reinforced it with inner tubes. I don't know how long that will last but I'll find something else when that gives out...*

4.

Bob, this is big. BIG! BIG! BIG! This is the most impossible mission. Now I know why! It is impossible, but I am actually doing it! WE are actually doing it! Thanks a million for everything!

I checked the news at six o'clock every night to see if anything remotely relative was reported; I read the *International Herald Tribune*. Luckly, the momentum of working hard in classes continued, as I was still riding the first wave on the Congo, certain of our work, with nothing left to do but wait it out. When I did have moments of worry, of concern out of my own distance and ignorance, I walked again the old tracks or the paths well behind Francis Hall, sometimes clear into Olean and on the dikes above the river behind the Topps

Supermarket. Joseph Conrad would simmer to the surface as if I had written his *Heart of Darkness* myself: Paths, paths everywhere; a stamped in network of paths spreading over the empty land, through long grass, through burnt grass, through thickets, down and up chilly ravines, up and down stony hills ablaze with heat, and a solitude, a solitude, nobody, not a hut. I passed several abandoned villages.

Joseph Conrad and I became good friends back in college. Henry Stanley, too. And Beryl Markham, Hemingway, Dineson. We all laughed together in my dorm, at the library, at Antonio's. Joe introduced us, and we all spent long nights searching deeper into Africa, into the Congo, until it took on a life of its own.

5.

To get to the source I bought a bicycle and put my gear on it and rode. It took forever and I had to stop a lot. Now, here on the river I have only a little bit more hard paddling before I get to smooth sailing. Then only a couple of more interruptions with rapids until Kinshasa. I am going to make it.

6.

Joe's last letter:

This will probably be my last adventure. After this there is no greater mountain to climb. The loneliness on the river can really make one stop and reflect on life. Where I've been. Where I'm going. It makes me realize how old I'm getting. And how young I'm not remaining. It makes me want to stop and be with my family for Christmas. It's been so long. It makes me want to stop and want to get started on a real life. It makes me realize what my father was saying when I left home this time. "When is it going to end?" It makes me realize how much I love my family and that I don't really belong here and I should return to where I belong and find some sort of future. A guy just came in and warned me to be out of Shaba by August. There's going to be a rebellion.

I wonder if anyone will appreciate (this river trip) other than myself.

I'm sitting here in Kolwezi waiting for my other camera to be sent out from Kinshasa and also healing my wounds. Hopefully these worms will disappear with this medicine I'm on. They are driving me nuts.

I've probably never had such a nice tan in my life due to sitting 12 hours a day in the sun for months straight, although there are many clouds. It rains every day. I've seen so many animals and so few people. I've gone weeks without a trace of man. Anyone. Whoever says the world is overpopulated is off his rocker. There are hundred of miles in this world with nothing.

At first the hippos and crocs made me nervous, but they always run (dive deep) when I approach. I never met an animal other than man that is dangerous.

Hopefully I'll be back stateside before school is out, but this trip is going much slower than I imagined it would. While having nothing to eat but raw fish for awhile I began to dream of the wonderful food at Hickey (dining all at St Bonaventure), and how I'd love to be a student back there just for the food.

It was taking longer than we anticipated, but he was still there, still paddling, and it brought back the reality of it all. Then, when people inevitably ask yet again how Fly is doing and if I had heard from him, I could say yes; I could smile and tell them what he said, certain to embellish the details. I left for home awaiting word to fly to Zaire. That summer I worked and I waited. It was a long, long summer. It would be quite some time before I understood a few unspoken truths of those days:

One, that Joe at just twenty-seven-years old was more terrified than he ever let on, and he second guessed himself more often than I knew.

Two, I could have talked him out of going. Despite what his father told me and others suggested, I came to know the deep reliance we had upon each other to get through those days of adjustment—me in a brand new place alone for the first time in three years, and Joe back home with no plans for the first time in three years—and I only recognized the nuances of our relationship and how we both weren't so much fixated on The Congo as we were both trying to find something to prove we were alive.

I could have stopped him from going. Only his mother understood that.

Phone call to Kohn residence, North Collins, New York:

"Mrs. Kohn, this is Bob Kunzinger. Have you heard from Joe?"

"I haven't. His father contacted the State Department in July after we spoke to you. They started a search. Your letter a few months ago indicated he should have been back by April or May?" It was late August, and I was back at school.

"Yes, but that was the best-case scenario," I said. "It would take very little to delay a trip like this."

"I thought you guys figured that into your planning. Why did you let him go, Bob? He would have listened to you."

"Some things can't be anticipated, like weather and him having to hold up for a bit in some village. He'd have no way of letting us know."

There was a long silence; long like it happens when you know the person on the other end of the phone wants to say something but changes her mind. "Please call when you hear from him," she said.

"I will. I'm back at Bona's now. You know, Mrs. Kohn, this isn't Joe's first disappearing act," I said.

His mother laughed. "True. This has happened before, a few times." When Joe left Africa after his Peace Corps duty, he took a freighter to Rio de Janeiro, not telling anyone of his departure or arrival times, where he was going, when he might arrive home. He spent time on the Amazon, in Belem. On his bike trip to South America, his transport from Panama to Columbia left him mostly out of touch with civilization. Simply because no one knew where he was didn't mean he was missing. No one worried that much.

Another letter was waiting for me at school in August, but it had been mailed the previous January, the same day as his last letter. I don't know why it would have taken nearly nine months to arrive except he gave it to a Peace Corp worker to mail, but that person wasn't near a city until the following summer. It used to work that way sometimes. I also don't know when it arrived at the college, but no earlier than about May 5th when I left for break. Still, no other letters were delivered.

In part:

I've seen animals of all kinds. Thousands of hippos, crocs, plus antelope, wild pigs, monkeys, leopards. No problems from any animals; they are all afraid of me... so far! This is going to take longer than we planned, but I will try like anything to finish about the time you are through with school. It's a great adventure, greater than either of us imagined. Sorry it took so long to write again, but this was the next village. I'm feeling pretty weak from some intestinal thing, but it will pass. Did you get the maps of the Amazon?!

A few months later, this letter:

> From: Embassy Kinshasa:
> To: American Consulate Lumbumbashi Party
> Embassy appreciates the efforts you have made to date in search for Joseph Kohn. We have not learned any new information regarding his whereabouts. We are making inquiries in other regions. Department contact with Kohn family negative, as we have all responses from neighboring posts. We are also inquiring with Kinshasa Immigration, though it is unlikely they will have any info on Kohn. All Peace Corps personnel have been alerted about search. We have also alerted aid personnel in Bukavu. Unfortunately neither embassy or Peace Corps has any more specifics than that provided in earlier cables.

I had told his parents that I told the State Department I thought they were looking in the wrong places. I offered them my maps but that went unanswered.

"Maybe he went back to Brussels," his mother said. But he hadn't. "Or maybe he is at some village helping them like he did in Brazil," she added.

"That's absolutely possible," I said, and we agreed to talk again soon.

No, it wasn't possible. Nothing in his life or the planning

pointed to such a conclusion, certainly not without contacting me or someone. The search, then, began by clarifying what we didn't know. He didn't return, he didn't contact anyone in Kinshasa. He didn't turn around and return to Kolwezi.

From: Embassy Kinshasa
Neither embassy nor Mel Adam of Peace Corps has any more specifics about Kohn's route than that provided in earlier cables. He has not contacted friends in Kinshasa who are holding his mail and personal belongings for him. It is possible Kohn may have abandoned his trip when he encountered difficulties and departed Zaire without contacting his friends.

No, this wasn't possible either. And this information worried me the most. I had sent money from gem sales, wrote letters about news and magazine outlets interested in his journey, indications of hope I thought he would have received to lift his spirits. His parents' letters, as well, remained in Kinshasa. He never made it to or sent work to Kinshasa, ever, on the entire journey, except at the start when he lost his belongings at a waterfall. And he did not abandon his trip. Not on purpose.

Phone call from Kohn residence, North Collins, NY.

"I don't see a point, Bob. Bob, we're sorry. Cole Young was here last week asking about him, and we all agreed he had to have perished. I wish one of us could have gone there just to talk to someone ourselves. Anyway. Thank you for everything, Bob, but we don't see a reason to look anymore."

Twelve

Nineteen

My students can often have the attention span of a lightning bolt. The plethora of distractions means measuring the material I need them to know against the amount of time they'll be aware I am in the room. This wasn't always the case.

In the early '80's, our dorm rooms had no phones, no televisions, no electronics of any kind. We talked to each other, played sports, drank. But if you didn't fit in you went out—sometimes to Niagara Falls, sometimes to Letchworth State Park, often just across the river to Merton's Heart. We had infinitely more time to think, to let our minds wander and sort things out. We were forced not to "find" answers but to figure them out on our own.

If you were nineteen years old with a tendency to let your mind wander anyway, waiting for a letter, a call, any information at all from the other side of the world is infuriating. In classes my junior year I'd listen and try and participate, but life quite quickly slipped back to the way it had been before Joe ever showed up; mundane information about subjects I'll never need. I sat one day in Dr. Francis Kelley's "Epistemology and Metaphysics" course and realized I couldn't even define the name of the course, let alone the philosophies we attempted to communicate. The material had little apparent relevance at that age, and it was blatantly absent of weather conditions, wildlife, village life, and river currents. More often than not I had to retrieve the notes from someone later even though I had been sitting right there.

Then in journalism class one day, the professor, Dr. Russell Jandoli, who happened to be my advisor, asked the class after we had turned in a paper about current issues and accuracy in reporting, "Where did you get your information?"

I couldn't remember. The Iranian hostage crisis when fifty-two Americans were being held hostage in Tehran had ended, and then President Ronald Reagan was in a verbal tennis match with Soviet Premier Mikial Gorbachev. My twenty-year-old mind thought I was being precisely wise when I said, "The stacks in the library, some tapes, and the New York Times." I said the last one with a nod of the head as if all students with as much expertise as I had would also nod; that "where else am I going to get it; what a dumb question" kind of nod.

"Mr. Kunzinger, you just referenced a building, a type of recording device and a newspaper. What are the book titles? Article titles? Author's credentials? How do I know you're not making it up? How do I know your sources aren't making things up?"

Then to everyone:

"Everyone, nothing is more important than the answer to this question: 'Where did you get your information?' This can mean the difference between accusations and libel, between getting published and getting fired, between, unfortunately truer than you care to know, between life and death."

For thirty-five years I've been telling nineteen-year-olds on the first day of class that "Where did you get your information?" is the root question from which all debate, discussion, and credibility develop. I tell them that it is absolutely true: a bad or questionable source can be the difference between life and death.

I left Dr. Jandoli's class with a clear understanding of what he was looking for, and I made it halfway to my dorm when I stopped in my tracks and wondered, not with a little rise in anxiety, where Joe and I got our information from. Sure, the maps are from the State Department, I thought, but medical research, astronomy, sustenance and survival issues were from various, unknown sources, pulled from dusty shelves . Some textbooks from faculty in various departments were helpful but dreadfully outdated. The most important information, of course, was about navigation and sustenance, village locations, with animals a close third. We felt confident any information in those areas, since it was gathered mostly from government sources including the State Department, the Peace Corps, and the World Health Organization, was solid. We are fine, I thought, as I headed again toward my dorm, stopping at the post for a quick second look in case a letter from Africa had arrived.

But when I got back to my room, Dr. Jandoli's, "Where did you get your information?" echoed in my brain as I glanced about the small space with the Congo maps against the wall and a tin of jewels on my desk. I thought about our long conversations about diseases, about animals, about the rain—"Gotta beat the rain," we said, but why? Where was the most accurate information about that? We read the works of every explorer who had ever dreamt of The Congo, first person account which certainly provided atmosphere and inspiration, but not expertise. Experience and expertise are not nearly the same thing. I can hear Dr. Jandoli emphasizing that while we may talk to someone who has been to Tehran a dozen times, he has no expertise on hostage negotiations, no knowledge of the opposition forces, no clue as to the readiness of allied forces. Yet the news was endlessly filled with such spurious information.

Yet isn't that exactly what we did for a year? Joe "had all the ingredients" but no true expertise in anything except animal husbandry. We studied languages and his three years there precluded the need to start from scratch but on a line running from novice to expert, he wasn't too much closer to expert than I was. It's no wonder, I realized, that I felt I was as ready for the trip as Joe; I probably was.

Where did we get our information? I said aloud to no one.

I walked to the river and waded across, hiked up the wooded slope to Merton's Heart and sat in the cool, damp pasture, looking back at the Allegheny, across the ball fields to campus, the bell tower, the library where a thousand years earlier Joe and I laughed quietly under dim desk lamps with students and faculty close by asking questions. His answers were all first person; his knowledge was all first-hand. In the world of accuracy and validation, we failed.

How do you find expertise about something no one has ever done?

I rationalized that we had done all we could, got as close as anyone could and closer, perhaps, than we ever imagined we could. We were ready, I decided, again. We had the maps, learned the astronomy, the languages, the topography, the survival means; we learned the political relationships between villages, between various groups of people; we learned to temper loneliness and to celebrate small victories; we learned about which areas had animals of concern and which had waters in which he was free to swim without worry.

We were so ready. Yet, little of the information came from any source that had enough value to feel secure. I suddenly knew with absolute conviction—even with the arrogance I carried at twenty-years-old—that Joe was completely unprepared to make this journey. The fledgling adventurer in me thought he knew better; the hopeful journalist in me made a better argument. Often it is the lack of information which proves an argument, and not going was winning hands down.

May came slowly and classes passed at some immeasurable pace. Each lecture less relevant than the previous, each day further from the adventure of planning the journey yet somehow not feeling any closer to its fruition. No calls from Kinshasa, no letters from Zaire, not a thing I could do about it either.

Before leaving for summer break I walked across the street to Antonio's one night and sat in the lounge. Dee was a true tender; he knew if I had something to say I would have said it, one way or the other, so he simply asked about my plans for the summer. Still, after we talked for about thirty minutes and I stood to leave without mentioning Joe or letters or calls, he appeared slightly disappointed. He knew, of course, my answer should have been, "This summer? I'll be in Zaire!" Instead, I told him I was returning to the hotel in Virginia Beach and I'd see him in August.

On a walk along the old railroad tracks I anticipated one ingredient neither of us had ever mentioned, and it was the x-factor to almost all adventures which push the limits of logic: Luck. No calculating mind who pushes themselves to the edge of reason to achieve a goal would ever realistically rely upon something as unpredictable as sheer luck, but that's exactly what we did. It would be lucky if the villages were still where he thought they were, lucky if the rains did what the "predictable patterns" suggested, lucky if he didn't get too ill for the medicines at hand, lucky if he simply didn't paddle past a pissed off Mother Hippo.

What does one do when waiting for news from far away and the expected time has come and gone? You wait. Summer came. It was hot and humid, and I canoed the Lynnhaven River in Virginia Beach more than I had before, somehow perhaps trying to vicariously finish the damn trip, paddle up to the backyard to hear my dad calling me, "Phone! It's long distance!" That didn't happen. Nothing did. Summer went.

Two years after Joe should have completed the trip, I graduated.

Curious men go prying into all sorts of places where they have no business.

—Joseph Conrad

Thirteen

Lost in the Present Tense

After college I move to Arizona, and I believe I see Joe in a record store. In Massachusetts at an Inn where I serve tables, a reservation comes in for a party of two, name: Joe Kohn. I am off work that night, but I show up anyway. I bring water to the table and say I know someone by the same name, but this couple is from Florida. I move to Pennsylvania and tend bar in Harrisburg. I go to work every day, go home every night. Life turns into a predictable, comfortable current, albeit completely unchallenging, and I stop thinking about Africa, sort of, about Coos Bay, mostly. *Maybe I'll go to grad school*, I think. Yet just as quickly I think again, *maybe not*. I was twenty-seven.

It is not because of Joe's disappearance that I find myself floundering; it would have happened anyway and in fact started long before Joe came to the college that Friday afternoon in February so long ago. I lacked that internal motivation so many others seemed to have been born with. No, it is because I can't find anything interesting to do with my life. My adulthood began by planning a tremendous adventure in the Congo which set me up for disappointment with everyday life, but I still hold that's not what happened. I was bored before that; I was easily distracted long before that.

Today, looking back, I might suggest I was looking for that dopamine rush we experienced virtually every single day for so long, and I could never find it. But truth impels me to admit I assumed Joe would eventually show up like he had before. His disappearance didn't truly seem like a death to me; he was simply not present. And this was at a time when communication with one's own parents might only happen sporadically at best, so it wasn't like I was expecting a weekly update from Joe. Not back then.

I move again. It turns out that what I am good at and have become used to is to move every three years or so, hundreds of miles away where I know absolutely no one. Been doing it since I'm fifteen. Eventually I tend bar again.

My girlfriend joins the Air Force, my cat runs away, and my car dies. I go to work to watch people root at the bar and drink until wallets are tapped and taps are empty. They spend in one afternoon what I might earn for the day if it rains. Sometimes a friend calls, an invitation, a temptation to spend an afternoon in a park. I used to criticize the customers who came in on a sunny Saturday to drink beer and sit and lie all afternoon, but I find myself now just feet away. And now Lieutenant Johnny needs another beer. He was drafted into this side-alley trench thirty years ago. He swallows fast and by the time I rest, maybe clean off the service area or wash glasses, he needs another; it drains me when he comes in.

Noise constantly filters from the kitchen, from the customers, from the glasses and ice. It all blends. I am part of the noise; I blend. After happy hour the shy construction worker sneaks away from the single men and bids me so-long; he wants to get home to his family. The man in the silk suit buys another scotch for the blond near the popcorn machine then must get home to his wife "before she turns into a royal bitch." I listen to all of this while I hold my hand on the patrons' arteries. I control the flow; I control the volume of their urine. I distill their precious blood into ten-ounce Jimmy Jones' Kool-Aid glasses. My co-worker, Walt, gets as irritated as me, has trouble hiding his disdain for drunks. "I hate this," he says to me. "Reminds me of something I can't put my finger on."

I sigh. "It's like being a freshman in college again."

The third scotch the silk suit man bought worked and he won't be going home to the bitch after all. Another old man is drinking to forget something distant and sour, and I see in him I might live long enough in spite of myself. He pushes a dime next to the glass and says he is going to enjoy the sun and I briefly remember "outside"; when I am behind the bar bar it is easy to forget "outside." There are no windows here, save some stained glass in the door, and even that is thick with beer-stein art making the light dark, like it is filtered through Guinness. Outside I can hear the cars idle, and I can hear the music as it rips up Third Street, girls with their hair combed out. They are on their edge. They sit on the hood pushing toward night, and the guys spend hours impressed by the sensual ritual of it and find purpose.

I stopped drinking when I started to tend bar, so sometimes I am unable to breathe, ready to dart into the late-night cold air and run jobless toward some distant land, pick up my feet and find myself in other places. Breathe again. But one man is watching the football game and he and Johnny get into a conversation about the importance of the instant replay, and then others in the bar disagree and an argument begins; an afternoon is dedicated.

This is what I've become.

The room spins and I sit at a stool while my boss's voice shatters even the sounds from the music and televisions and the commotion of a table of drunk guys in the corner, and I want to look away but there is no "away," there is only here, and I slip some each day, drowsy with my duties. Without anyone noticing right in the middle of this tavern. I drained all the life out of this motionless soul. It isn't the incomplete journey that created my lethargy, not any moment or situation. I simply am not even remotely interested in anything. I always figure what I'm looking for I'll find on the next move, in some other place. It seems I'm always looking in the wrong place for answers. The owner asks if I can work a double the next day. I'm not doing anything else anyway.

I go out into the night air to find something familiar, something other than life behind bars. I bend my neck toward the cold, square sky just above the rooftops, void of celestial light, and feel nothing. Even in this late night-early morning vastness, traffic seems to flow and the air flinches at vibrations coming from apartments and stereos and restaurants. A group of teens stands outside a twenty-four-hour drug store and wait for something to happen. They fall silent when I walk by, and a small part of me wonders if they're contemplating how much cash I might have on me after a double shift, but a larger part of me doesn't give a rat's ass what they do. So, I ride out of the city.

A year passes. Same routine, same barren year, only the next one, and I remain absolutely lost. Once again it is late winter and the street is more brown slush than white snow, and warm days battle with the cold nights making the season unruly, moody. After work one night I walk to a lake near my home in the country and I wade into the water in the cold evening pitch. I wake the next morning on a nearby bench and know that in three more hours I have to get back to the city and do it again when a voice from somewhere else—not inside, exactly, but not ghostly either. I'm alone, and it feels more than sounds like a voice from a passing friend, or from a reoccurring dream, and it whispers *"or not."*

The next morning I call in sick. "You don't sound sick," Nick the manager tells me. *But I am*, I think, *sick and tired.* "I think I have a case of worms," I tell him, laughing to myself, and hang up. I need to do something. Anything. The phone is in my hand and my hand is on the table as I look out my window into the quiet country street. There is snow. I can hear Nick again, "Bob!! You don't sound sick!"

Three hours later in the Capital City Mall outside Harrisburg, Pennsylvania, I spot a world map in the window display of a travel agency and a banner claiming they can get us anywhere.

Let's simplify this: I know I've got to do something with my life or I'm going to disappear. So, I buy the ticket to visit a college friend who lives in Senegal who I had been writing and who knew all about Joe's Congo trip. A few letters earlier she told me to visit her. I make an appointment at the Hershey Medical Center to get my shots and malaria pills, I head to the Senegalese Embassy in Washington for my visas, I go to West Africa.

Fourteen

Acclimation

I stand on the airport runway having departed the twelve-seat plane as the blazing sun starts its decline across the eastern plains. Passengers scatter for the few buses waiting to bring them to the city while taxi drivers barter for riders. I pick up my bag and toss it over my shoulder and walk toward town. A hazy still makes the African sky seem like stretched canvas; the sun impressionistic—closer. And I can hear the ocean very silently like a whisper. A kid tries to sell me a can of pineapple juice. I look around and shake my head. *Fucking Africa*, I think.

Note: I should have started here. I've messed with this manuscript for three dozen years now, adding, subtracting, wondering if anyone would even care. But through all of it the most difficult decision has always been where to start.

This is where it starts.

In Dakar after a few days, I meet with a man I contacted at the American Express office in the city who arranges my transportation to Zaire, but I tell him I am not sure when I will be ready to leave, and that I am going to spend a few weeks in the east. He only needs two days' notice, he tells me. He says to simply stop by when I return to the city.

After some time acclimating myself to this new world in Dakar, I rise before dawn and buy space on a seven-seater van to make the long journey to a small village across the country with my friend . Dust blows in the broken window, and we make motionless time, watching the countryside fade as the day progresses. It is mostly barren, a few trees. Villagers herd sheep and cattle, and a few camels cross the road looking for undiscovered vegetation. The road itself is somewhat paved, mostly not, almost twenty feet wide and chewed at the sides, swallowed by the desert. In some places entire pieces of pavement have been digested. The sun reaches higher, stretching the intensely blue sky to its extremes when the driver pulls off for a rest and I take in the silence, absorb the quiet.

We sit amidst the dust and ruins and after some time children serenade us, chanting the Koran. The sun sits directly above, and I think for a moment it might drop. A lady stands before an open doorway, dry, dusty, her lips cracked. The river is dry. The well is dry. The sky is dry. The lady lets out a sigh. *Has God died?* I swear I hear her say as tears moist dust on her child's lips.

We sit on the fingertips of the Sahara, eating rice, drinking hibiscus juice and we listen to the children sing for money. A soft breeze chases away about thirty minutes before the engine roars to life and we eagerly load the van and continue. Young boys run alongside with open hands stretched, still singing. It is all they learn; it is their life. For the rest of the trip we load and unload passengers as the landscape becomes more desolate, thirsty. But first, after everyone else gets in the van for the final stretch, I wait. They call in French for me to come, and slowly I do.

I drink it all in; swallow the grace and history and raw, naked presence of my surroundings. *There is nothing about this place to fear*, I think. I take a long, unhurried, advent breath, and feel my pulse slow to an equatorial pace and know, finally, perhaps for the first time since that first year in college, that this is where it begins.

At the village late at night we drink tea with a hint of mint and sugar stirred in the dark leaves. Traditionally, at least here in Senegal, the host pours the pot from high above a few glasses, no drops missing. First the chief or a guest or someone with a birthday will slurp it from the rim of the glass until it is empty, and then more is poured from the pot's high perch and the glass is passed to the next person around the fire. The tea is potent. By eleven PM my African friends, whose nature and genes defy caffeine, sleep peacefully while I, well, simply can't. I sit for hours and reread my letters, examine the maps I had once again copied from the State Department maps, pulling them out of their plastic sheaths. In a few weeks I must return to Dakar to meet my new friends and begin this journey to Bukavu, Zaire, and eventually Kolwezi, about four thousand miles south.

This tea has opened my veins, so I sit up and read about traveling through the region, the flights, the buses. The tea ceremony is called Attaya. The first round is strong and bitter, the second sweeter with a hint of mint, and the third round sweet and minty. It mirrors friendship, which grows over time to reflect how the longer we know each other the sweeter the relationship. What happens most during Attaya, however, is talk. We consume conversation. We talk about the rain, if there is any, the wind, which is more common, the oppressive sun. And the villagers return to their natural spaces, rest or sleep peacefully. I leave the fire wondering if I am ready to leave.

I have no ebbing sense of tiredness, no headaches when I don't drink. No. When I first arrived in the village, the chief looked like God; he is taller than most, well over six feet anyway, and dark, with long, thin, strong arms, and a white robe that wraps down his legs. He is ancient and eternal. He is Achilles, he is Gandhi. He is Mohammad. Even when doing nothing at all, this man has complete determination about him.

"What is your purpose here?" he asked me in those first days. "Why are you here?"

"To see what's out here; to meet people like you." I said, and he nodded. "To have a look around," I added. "To see more stars. You have more stars than we do at home." We laughed and that first night he poured tea in some beautiful and ritualistic way. I had traveled often, but never before had I felt so safe, so in touch with a group of people, and so welcomed. I wondered what life here would have been like had the Europeans not decided for them what their future held. At the same time, I could not imagine a more genuine existence. I stayed.

The chief, Besitio, asks a series of questions akin to "How are you with the sun? How are you with the wind? How are you with your sleep" and so on, and to each one you answer, alternatively, "Jam Tan" or "Moe Doom Day" (spelling is mine, phonetically, from the Pulaar language). Both of these mean "I am at peace," but in a simple way—it is the Pulaar equivalent of "I'm fine." But eventually he will ask something like "How are you with everything?" to which you reply, "Ya Wur," or "I am at Peace," but it is a grandeur peace, a complete, all-encompassing peace. Ya Wur.

Often, I walked outside the village, wide awake, and let myself blend with the sound, the lack of sound, the immersion of my entire self in the liquid of African sound and listen to what was missing. It took a complete opening of my senses to finally tune in to what wasn't there: No sound of blame. No sound of disillusionment. No sound of hypocrisy. All I could hear in that tight-rope awakeness was that one passing moment; the complete absorption of now. It took an absolute absence of civilization to feel completely aware and connected. It was right then I understood without a doubt that I never could have talked Joe out of going, not after even this small moment of time on this continent. No one could have talked me out of it.

There I was.

It wasn't the tea. Sugar and caffeine had nothing to do with this. I had made my peace. I no longer felt the need to search, to discover something else. What I thought was "more" turned out only to be "different." I told my friend I had to leave. Before me lay this space, the unreachable horizon, the vast imagination of Africa, spread like distant but promising hope. It is that quick but fleeting moment of clarity that makes me sit up straight and watch the increasing soft glow on the eastern plains. It is the persistence of some primitive way of life that had no chance of surviving but survives anyway which finds me at peace.

I bid my farewell to Claire and the village chief and his wife, as well as all my new friends in the village. We took a charette to the larger village of Matam, and I purchased a space on a seven-seater van to head back to Dakar. I was the only non-African, the only English-speaking man, and we rolled quietly across the barren sub-Saharan desert. After introductions, no one spoke to anyone else, and we stared ahead at the mirages of fresh water in the dirt road. I think about simply going home. Just being here seemed to be enough to understand what I was hoping to find. But I keep thinking about something so obvious: I am in Africa;

I am on the very continent whose exact center and one of its most infamous places, the Congo, I studied as astronauts might study their flight patterns. The notion of going south to the Congo brought me such peace, despite enough time having had passed to know "missing" slipped well past "presumed dead" some time before. Still, I knew there was still something down there for me to discover that I should so easily yield the entire impetus for coming to begin with.

The van rocked west when at midday three uniformed Mauritanians "patrolling" across their border stopped us in a much-too-barren spot and demanded we exit the van. Our driver seemed more unsettled than he had been. He tried to negotiate with them, but this was not a sale, this wasn't routine. They pulled our bags from the roof. When they found mine, they pulled out my clothes, my camera and film, my medicines, a few items of some value, and they ordered us to stand with our heads against the van. They kept their guns ready.

Several of the passengers objected, and the driver tried to wrestle my bag back from one of the soldiers until the man pointed his gun at him, and the other two pointed theirs at us, and we all remained absolutely still and silent. I thought that if I were going to kill a van full of people there is nowhere else on the globe I'd find better suited than right here. These guys were good. I hoped they did not check inside the van where my small bag of papers, maps, and other essential information sat beneath the thick, ripped cushion.

Everything slowed down. It was well over one hundred degrees out and the heavy air moved like a thicker version of itself. My eyes took in the action frame by frame, like a projector moving slow enough to see the breaks in the strips of film. The heat from the exhaust lifted into my face, my forehead pressed against the van's open side door, and behind us the three men said nothing to each other but continued to rummage through our goods.

One of the men came and stood next to me and stared at the back of my neck. He just stood there, close enough for me to smell him, to feel his breath on my back. I didn't turn around and he went about his business when a tall, slender Senegalese man beside me whispered, "We must yield to these gentlemen."

I was standing against the van wondering why we were still there. The driver had been pleading with these bandits to let us go, but they didn't reply. It got quiet and I decided that if they were going to kill us, they most likely would have by now; and anyway, they had what they wanted. To me their silence signified approval. I suggested we all just get in the van and leave, but at first only the driver agreed.

I looked at the tall man next to me. "Yield," he had said. "To give over possession of, to give up, to surrender, to concede."

To not follow through, I thought.

While history shows the ancestors of these people often fought with dignity and diligence to their death, so many of these people know little else except to yield. I turned to the three men and took one step in their direction, noticed their guns resting aimlessly on their laps as they shared my possessions, and I turned back and climbed in the van. By this time the van driver was behind the wheel and shifting into gear while the rest hesitantly boarded. We rode off. They never reached for the guns, they never looked up. They never cared.

We drove without talking for some time before he pulled over, and we all got out and breathed again. My stomach sat somewhere near the engine fan ready to be shredded, and one man in the back covered his mouth as if he might get sick.

The tall man asked me how I was.

"Ya Wur," I said. He smiled. I laughed that loud growing sort of laughter one does that is a combination of nervous energy and complete relief. We just kept laughing. A boy ran up from his small nearby village to sell us juice. His mother came and talked to the driver, then she left and returned with food and water. We drank tea and talked about where we had been in the east and what our business was west in Saint-Louis, or down in Dakar where I was headed, but none of us talked about the three men or the guns.

A few hours after we abandoned the bandits we arrived in Saint-Louis, and the next day I made it south to Dakar. I went to the Peace Corps center across from the Grand Mosque where my friend had let me store some things, and then it hit me; the guns, the idling van and the heat. My stolen belongings, my severed nerves; the crime that became Africa; the beauty and loss that defined half a millennium. I was never more convinced I needed to simply get the hell out of there and go home.

This is our journey! I remembered Joe saying.

I sat alone in a small room used as a library where the tall windows were open to let in the ocean breeze, and I rested, still shaking somewhat from the three men and their guns and how we climbed into the van waiting to hear gunshots. The others might have waited all day, I thought. It is their way, to wait, to follow the natural pace of each incident. Thinking too much about it made me shake violently, so I took a sip of tea and reached over my head for a book, any book, anything to focus on.

I have an idea, he said.

Bob, I need your help, he said.

I looked at the spine of the book. It was Tennyson. I opened at random to "Ulysses," wherein Tennyson writes:

> Though much is taken, much abides; and though
> We are not now that strength which in the old days
> Moved earth and heaven; that which we are, we are,
> One equal-temper of heroic hearts,
> Made weak by time and fate, but strong in will
> To strive, to seek, to find, and not to yield.

I look out the window and for the first time in hours feel I could breathe on my own. I put the book back, take my belongings out of my friend's locker, and walk through the market to the American Express office to tell them I am ready to head south when they are.

This is my trip.

Fifteen

Transition

With the determined assistance of the good people at the American Express office in Dakar, I catch what turns out to be three flights to get from Dakar to Kinshasa to Bukavu. After a long night in a dusty motel, I wake to find a South African man looking much like an ex-marine waiting in the lobby. We get in his truck filled with dry goods and gas cans, and we leave on what will be a six-hundred-mile ride on rough roads, where there are roads. After some time, we stop in a small village and are serenaded by more children's choirs chanting the Koran. A lady stands before an open doorway for thirty minutes. Just stands there. I know this because we sit here as long; longer. Nearby a child falls and cries. I'm starting to get restless, however, and I tell my driver we need to leave. I need to beat the rains.

Sixteen

In Country

I sat in the passenger seat of the brown, International pickup, finally oblivious to the bumps and bangs of the only partly paved road to Kolwezi. People walked along carrying bags and babies and the best of the little they owned. It would be another decade before the Hutu and Tutsi genocide in Rwanda to the east, but even now, refugees streamed west on the roads toward anywhere else. My South African driver, Brian, transported materials from the Kisangani airport to Bukavu and Kolwezi once every few weeks. He carried canned goods, rice, millet, blankets, medical supplies, and bottled water. His tanned face and blond hair separated him visually, and his South African accent separated him politically from just about anyone. To be clear, we were obvious travelers. We drove through rugged and wretched conditions and the dirt and dust lifted through the floorboard and we banged down the road.

It had been a few years since I received Joe's last letter. Just a few months since I was able to get my hands on embassy letters about Joe's disappearance. Those who searched knew what they were doing, knew who to contact, and the truth is it would not have been difficult to find someone who might have seen a blond haired American.

So I was frustrated. I had the marked maps of the Congo and the tributaries. I had the maps marked with destinations, stopping points, notes, possible hiding places should troubles arise. I had the original State Department maps we spread out on library tables and had memorized each turn, each waterfall.

When Joe first planned the trip, he wrote to the State Department explaining his background and his intentions. They sent him these seven maps, each about three feet by three feet. One represented the entire nation, the rest focused on regions. We copied the maps and slid them into plastic pouches for protection. I kept the originals. Still, it took a Freedom of Information Act to obtain the letters stating they didn't know where he was.

I held the letters in my lap in a tattered envelope covered in cracking yellow tape. Every word and punctuation mark, I memorized. Brian looked at the letters. "You really think you'll learn anything while you're here?" His arms jolted about like bungee cords, holding the wheel so as not to get tossed through the rusted roof. We had been on smooth, paved roads for some time, but now we moved south, close to Kolwezi.

"No," I said, exiting the conversation instead of starting an entirely new one which had nothing really to do with Joe at all, though I didn't understand that at the time. He swerved to skirt a woman walking in the road. We pulled over. "I'm not an idiot," I laughed, and he looked at me. "He's dead, and I won't find him."

He was quiet for a moment. "Then...?"

My face cracked beneath days of dirt and a two-week-old beard. I wore worn, green pants made in Senegal and a blue UNC Chapel Hill t-shirt. I carried a backpack with journals, money, medicine, a plane ticket, and some letters.

I had the address of a Peace Corps house in Kolwezi where they were expecting me and where I would stay for a few days. I had the maps with details about where to go after Kolwezi, all the way to Banana on the Atlantic. The last time I was involved like this in these areas I was just a nineteen-year-old kid. Sitting in that truck bouncing through the green hills of Zaire made those days of my late teens seem decades earlier. He was a different person.

"Why?" he asked.

Because I have the maps.

Because yesterday or the day before or last year I kept wondering what happened to abort a perfectly planned, organized, calculated trip not just on the Congo but to Coos Bay. Because it should have worked out; there shouldn't have been any problems. Because newspapers ran stories, radio hosts interviewed Joe, sometimes me, about the trip. Because his father wanted to know what happened to his son, because Conrad said it couldn't be done and Stanley said it could but only with a hundred men.

Because Joe's letter said he was through the hard part, that this was "Big!" and because his boat was in terrible shape, his spirits were low, and he was fighting a case of worms. Because missing is unacceptable, like an incomplete grade or an unfinished manuscript. All paths were marked and clear, measured, because life weighed practically nothing at all, and we had energy to burn. Because I needed that energy again. Because I had no other plans anyway. Because Coos Bay, Oregon, was just too far and bartending wasn't way too close.

Because I had nothing else to do.

Somewhere between Bukavu and nowhere we were pulled over at some seemingly random check point. Brian rolled to a stop and answered questions in French. They gave him a clipboard, and he put his identification on it, signed a paper and gave it back. Then the guard looked through Brian's window at me and asked some questions, some of which I recognized, others Brian gave me a head's up about, and one or two which puzzled even him. What kind of weapon did I carry? Did I work for a U.S. Agency? How long would I be in Zaire? Had I been in any other countries? They pointed us off the road and we got out of the truck. They gently searched the truck while another guard looked at my passport. He asked me something in French while Brian was in the back of the truck with the first guard, but I didn't understand. He pushed me toward a chain link fence, and I tripped, the ragged edge of the fence piercing my right cheek. A thin line of blood ran to the corner of my mouth and down my chin, and Brian yelled at him in French and told me to get in the truck. We left.

"He wanted money," he said. He looked at me a long time. "You've got some balls to be here."

"It wasn't supposed to be like this," I said, and Brian nodded.

After a while he said, "It *wasn't* like this. Not until recently."

We drove on to Kolwezi.

As we entered Kolwezi, my lips were dry and I drank water and looked around at the colors of the clothes of the hordes of people—red and yellow, green, teal blue—the brightness contrasted with, even mocked, the barren, emaciated landscape, or at the very least directly opposed my mood. Everything was green and brown, alive and hopeless; this was a city, not a village, the river was a place of commerce, not adventure. Nothing seemed right.

I had contact with a PC volunteer named Mark whose best friend had been a volunteer when Joe was here last, and he knew the story of what happened before Joe pushed into the river to the west of Kolwezi. I'd be at his door soon. I wanted to spend a few days near the Lualaba, maybe buck upstream for a day or two, possibly more, eyeball the shoreline. I'd follow the blue cheese dressing lines and the tomato sauce borders as far as I could. I knew the area, knew the dangers, knew to keep quiet and where to go next.

I was so ready.

Seventeen

How to Die in the Congo

First of all, to this day Joe is officially only "missing," though his family had a memorial service, and all references to him in relatives' obituaries note "the late Joseph Kohn." And while I only once, very briefly suggested to Joe that we need to anticipate what to do if he gets lost, I certainly wondered more than a few times how those of us at home might respond to the slight possibility of missing. Death at the very least is concrete. It keeps our attention because of what we call an "ending." We despise death for its finality, but we don't avoid it for the sheer concrete truthfulness it carries. There is weight in death, and clarity. Closure. In a paradoxical way, it is the ultimate security. It is too real to dismiss. One can't be "kind-of" dead. It's conclusive. I came here for some conclusion.

But when missing enters the mix, the direction of the narrative remains muddled among the infinite number of inconclusive outcomes. *Lost in the jungles; living in a village; Ebola; malaria; dysentery; the Crocodile Men of the Congo.*

The variables are exhausting. A croc can kill, but a hippopotamus won't even chew. Large, snapping bites and the limbs sink to the river bottom for other animals to devour.

Villagers kill Joe because he is a mercenary. Rebels kill him because he is not. The sun bakes. The night chills. The river bends and turns then twists into a thousand branches lit by nothing but moonlight, when there is a moon. Some tributaries travel thousands of miles and turn back on themselves, a labyrinth circling toward death. The river is the large intestines, twisting and spinning toward an evacuation that no one will discover. He could be anywhere, which is to say, essentially, he is nowhere to be found.

For a year before he left, we "trained" on the college campus where I was a freshman and from where he had graduated five years earlier. I would quiz him on his medical knowledge and treatment procedures. In most of the industrial world, death often comes with warnings; that is, prediction is common. EEGs. MRIs. CT Scans. Even cancer patients go through treatment. But in Africa, like many parts of this vast planet with still so much unchartered territory, death broadsides its victim. Death lies beneath the surface, only its eyes revealed, camouflaged by our confidence that we're well prepared. Death waits, searches for the vulnerable spot. It comes in large forms, like three-ton hippos, eighteen-feet-long crocs, rebels on the move.

It comes, too, in microscopic armies. Consider the parasites. During our research, these lilliputian terrorists remained part of our daily dissection of "modes of death." Schistosomiasis wins as the worst, of course. Water-borne flatworms carry the disease. In labs, they're called schistosome. In the jungle, a person doubles over while worms too small for the human eye to see devour his insides. I thought of Saint-Exupery: "What is essential is invisible to the eye." So is what's lethal.

These schistosome insurgents enter the body from a river's surface. Because of them, the World Health

Organization warns against paddling in fresh water. In the long term, exposure to them increases reports of bladder cancer by thirty-two times the rate in America. In the short term, however, acute infection causes temporary paralysis of the legs. Schistosomiasis itself is unlikely to kill. It's the animals, dehydration, reptiles, dysentery, hostile strangers, and other fatal combinations that transform a sick adventurer into vulnerable prey. Even if paralysis doesn't set in, lethargy and weakness can compromise safety.

We knew this.

We knew malaria posed itself as a problem since Joe contracted it before, rendering him more susceptible. His little orange pills ran out once and he had all the symptoms and problems associated with it, like fevers, shivering, pain in the joints, headaches, and vomiting. But treatment was readily available to him at the time. However, without treatment, death is common. Malaria is the anopheline mosquitoes' fault. They hang out near stagnant water and kill one child in the world every thirty seconds. In Africa today, the death rate for malaria far exceeds that of AIDS. The convulsions alone can kill since a child's body can shake so violently that the organs simply stop functioning. More than ninety percent of malaria cases are in sub-Saharan Africa, and deaths top about one million each year. Without medical attention, those otherwise treatable symptoms evolve into convulsions and coma. But carrying pills is easy so concern of malaria remained on our back burner.

Still, as a freshman at college my introduction to earth science, astronomy, biology, foreign languages, and geography came not from fifteen credit hours a semester; no, my exposure to the ways of this earth came after class in the library with Joe, at the river, at a local reservoir.

We would be prepared; it was that easy. Joe received

the yellow fever vaccination followed by many others. He knew to cook his meat and fish well, but somewhere between Lumbumbashi and Kolwezi, when he lost everything, including matches, going over falls, he ate fish dried in the sun on rocks. We prepared for this, too. We caught bass in the Allegheny River, dried it on rocks in the sun and ate it. We studied the fish of the Congo regions and learned that boiling most species avoids possible diseases.

Our vocabulary didn't include HIV and AIDS in 1981. No, we had another new entry in the entomological soup: Ebola. It remains one of the most virulent diseases known to humanity and causes death in about ninety percent of its victims. The symptoms include a sudden onset of fever, muscle pain, headaches and sore throat. One might seem to simply have the flu until the rash spreads and the kidneys shut down. Then the liver stops cleansing the blood, which by now courses through the bowels and urinary track. At this point, the internal organs literally liquify, and death is welcome. It is, luckily, a predominantly north Zairean problem, but people in remote African jungles do not readily report incidents of disease. When the west is aware of twenty new cases of Ebola breaking out in Uganda and the DRC, more remote cases along desolate regions of river tributaries remain unreported. Usually, one contracts Ebola by contact with the blood or semen of an infected person. However, transmission also occurs by handling dead chimpanzees, like those west of Kolwezi. Recent studies show that some bats carry the disease without dying, like the bats prevalent in central Africa.

Ebola kills, but so can a slight fever, even a common cold. What knocks a person onto a couch in suburban Buffalo can kill in rural Africa. It isn't the disability that poses the problem: hepatitis B, malaria, and others, while dangerous, can be cured. But in remote regions, the symptoms themselves can expedite death. Lethargy leaves one exposed to the elements. Tiredness, diarrhea and general sleepiness and weakness, while inconvenient at home, become critical when attempting to avoid animals that snap humans in two, reptiles that kill by a mere scratch, or hostile humans defending themselves against some unknown intruder.

Hell, just sleeping allows animals like the hippopotamus time to terrorize. Joe talked of their gentleness. Upon further study it seems their nonchalance is borne from confidence. Their lack of interest in humans results from having no fear at all. Hippos maintain a mostly vegetarian diet, consisting of grasses. But bulls grow to about eight thousand pounds and still remain graceful in the water. They sink to the bottom and run along, sometimes alone, sometimes in groups of up to thirty. During the mating season, territorial males use their long canines as weapons, snapping the enemy, including human, in two. Experts consider these animals among the most dangerous in Africa. Hippos don't sweat blood, as rumored in decades past, but they do spill plenty. Someone resting because of some ailment, or simply sleeping in the reeds of a riverbed during mating season, might cause a disturbance and not move fast enough to escape this graceful swimmer twice the weight of a Jeep Cherokee. Hippos can climb steep embankments fast, and snap in half or trample to death anything between them and their destination.

Research revealed comical dangers as well, particularly the "Crocodile Men from the Congo." What should be a title for some B movie is a reality check to those traveling to the south of Kinshasa. Villagers and police considered six tribal chiefs in possession of a mystical ability to turn themselves into crocodiles. They were arrested for killing thirty-three people. One confessed to eating five people during the previous fifteen years. Some Buma region fisherman left his village because he claimed he could identify the crocodile men and he feared them. He described them as monsters with human legs, crocodile faces and other features.

Real crocodiles devour. They hide in mud, in water, in grass, and chase, snap and swallow prey. The locking jaws of these eighteen-feet-long Jurassic remnants might snap a weak human too close to the river. They grip the body, crushing the spine, the neck, the skull, popping it and dragging it under a rock or riverbank to tenderize for later consumption. Crocs are a problem all along the Congo. Fishing has depleted their food supply. Drought has forced more people to the river, and once there, those people kill animals normally eaten by the crocs. And this food-supply depletion doesn't consider that conservationists who fight to protect the carnivores are leaving humans more susceptible to their hunt.

Reptiles, too, pose a threat. Dozens of snake species live along the riverbanks and in the water. Some cause no harm. Others debilitate a victim enough to leave that person susceptible to other dangers. Some snakes bite to paralyze and then kill within seconds, minutes at most. A person eating dried fish, weak from dehydration, might be bitten and then suffocate from muscle contraction. Other prey would devour him in time like the African rock pythons prevalent in the region and which can grow to a reported thirty feet. These coiling monsters eat goats, crocs, and humans. In 1958 in what was then Rhodesia, elephant tracker K. Krofft killed a rock python and found a six-foot croc inside. The Congo tributaries are their home. It's common practice that when a child is caught in this coil, the villagers nearly always allow the snake to crush the screaming child to death rather than jump in to help and certainly die as well.

People are more dangerous. Rwandan rebels wouldn't gather and wreak havoc with their sick, animal-like behavior from the border to Bukavu until the nineties, but just before Joe returned to Africa in the early eighties, rebel forces had emerged twice from Angola. Belgian paratroopers quickly ousted these Katangan insurgents, but some rebels continued to invade when Joe reentered the Shaba Province.

My God, the terrain alone kills. This earth of ours is not designed for human manipulation. The river is dangerous the entire 2,720 miles, but most hazardous after the meeting of the Lualaba and the Luvua rivers. From there water flows a thousand miles to Stanley Falls, north of the equator. But thousands of islands, some spanning ten miles, run along this long stretch, which under excellent conditions might take months to traverse. Several stretches of the river are altogether unnavigable. Waterfalls, as well, can surprise a solo traveler. One such falls, the Kiobo, on the Lufira tributary, pours down from almost thirteen hundred feet. West of Kolwezi, the river moves into a sort of lake-region where poor navigation can lead to an endless maze through jungles and smaller rivers, most of which humans have never mapped. This is Conrad's *Heart of Darkness*.

But the planning, the anticipation, ignited a spark in me which refused to be doused by worry of what might happen. He was twenty-seven; I was not yet twenty, and we were alive to the core. What a time it was, cutting up sun-dried fish we caught in the Allegheny River, laughing about the previous night's antics; conversations at Antonio's Italian Restaurant across from campus when faculty associated me with adventure and daring, and students counted me among the few that didn't belong there. The entire restaurant was always engaged when Joe and I showed up and he talked about his adventures in Africa, or stories of when he rode a bike from Buffalo to Brazil.

One night, Joe flipped over a soiled place mat and used tomato sauce and blue cheese dressing to draw a map of the Congo River. He looked up at me and said, quite seriously, "I have an idea, and I need your help."

Those were two different people; undeveloped characters in a bad movie I saw many years earlier.

Eighteen

The Congo River

The Congo River system is the most expansive in Africa. Some parts reach several miles wide and carry a volume of water second only to the Amazon. In other areas, rapids and waterfalls block navigation. The sudden descent of the river creates hydroelectric power potential greater than the power found anywhere else on the planet. The Congo cuts through mountain passages and hills throughout the provinces. Much of the river is so thick with trees along its shores, leaning in, tilting toward collapse, that resting on shore is not as simple as pulling to the side. The river near to the villages remains the source of food and water, bathing. It is a playground for children, a means of employment for adults, a bathroom for everyone. And, of course, near the larger towns and cities, such as Lumbumbashi, Kolwezi, and Bukavu, industry prevails, rendering a single man in a raft to an insignificant transient desiring again the more dangerous wild of the wooded shores. Most of the southern extension of the Lualaba River and as well as the lakes on the other side of this remote frontier drain north into the Nile Basin. This is what David Livingstone, and later Henry Stanley, searched for. Just south of this region where the Lualaba artery seeks the Congo is where Joe was last headed.

When one invests time and energy, heart and, quite literally, life into a place, it becomes theirs. I hear references to The Congo River on news stations or other outlets, and my emotional instinct is to think *Oh, they're talking about my river.*

Joe was correct from the start: This was always our trip. I secured a ride west out of the city to a rural area along the river. My guide and I got out of the car, walked through a park, along a road between some small buildings, and down a small hill to an embankment.

Mark told me that his friend Chris met Joe when he arrived at the village late, well after dark. "He saw him in the morning, and he looked like crap," he said. Dire Straits "Why Worry" played on some tape deck nearby. "A couple of them told him to ditch it, or at least get a new boat, but he wanted to push it. He said he would wait for some packages of supplies, letters, a camera, to arrive from Kinshasa, but when they told him that could be a few weeks, he decided to leave."

"Chris said he wouldn't have put that raft in a pool," he added. I still think about Chris, this guy who spent a few days with Joe more than four decades ago, yet because he is the last one to see Joe that I have ever had contact with, he is now part of my narrative, included in this vocabulary alongside Antonio's, Fly, Congo, inextricably linked to that time.

"He went in about here," Mark said, pointing. We stood on the shore. "He was pretty weak," Mark said. We both looked west. Odd how I had this sense that I knew better what was out there than he did. "Have you ever traveled out there?" I asked. He said only by vehicle but not on the river. It was the first time I even thought about there being roads here, no matter how battered they were, I always only envisioned the river.

Joe was here, at this spot, and he must have been emaciated, like a refugee leaving again for safer places. He fought a case of worms, and it was his birthday, January fourth. He might have stood at this very spot telling some children of his trip so far. *It was tough at first,* he would have told them, *and the villages are gone. The Congo starts somewhere near Mumena, near the Zambian border. Then I headed through Lake Nzila into the Lualaba region.*

He probably tried to be just as enthusiastic as when I last saw him, but his exuberance would have been a thin disguise for his illness and exhaustion. His raft was in poor condition, held together by the inner tubes of a bike. Did one of the tubes give out a few days later, bringing him to his death? His last journey may have ended because of inner tubes, which, ironically, carried him on his first journey ten thousand miles to South America.

I stared a long time toward the west, then waded in, slowly at first then with more confidence. The water tugged at my sneakers. Joe wore sandals made from tire treads. I wondered where they were now. When I waded in just knee deep, I stopped and wondered how far he got. The trees bent toward the water and men fished and spread nets. To the east was the city of Kolwezi with its seeming safety and buildings and market. To the west was wilderness and the mystique of my imagination. About me were men who must have worked these waters most of their lives. Did they watch Joe paddle by? Did they wave? Maybe he traveled for weeks before some wide tributary teased him off course. Perhaps after just a few days he became too weak to continue. It might not have mattered to him whether he was sick or in danger. It wouldn't have mattered to me. The water ran up my thighs as a small canoe moved behind me. I wanted to turn and see him standing on the shore, laughing, shocked, wondering what the hell I was doing in Africa. I wanted that so bad. Two teenagers stared at me from the shore. When this all started, I was their age.

How far did he get beyond here before something happened? Did animals attack? Could anyone hear? Did he become too weak to continue, to come back, to call for help? Did he get lost amidst the rivers and brooks, too far into the heart of darkness?

I remembered the stairwell, when the taxi came. I remembered the nights at Antonio's and faculty sitting around talking to me, accepting me as equal, listening to Joe's stories which were still then in retrospect; no one yet knew of our plans.

I thought of being fifteen years old and the tennis courts in Virginia Beach.

I watched the water flow across rocks and probably bones toward the equator carrying no apparent proof of death of my friend despite the unlikelihood of any other outcome. But "missing" is unacceptable, and as is often the case, the lack of information concerning what happened to him pulled me like a powerful current into that dark distance.

Like any narrative about wilderness and adventure, the spirit of place takes over, and I finally understood why he continued past here, despite his intestinal illness, his resulting weakness, and his indefinite sense of what to expect next. The Congo is enticing; it teases you into believing it is safe and protecting and eternal, that nothing could possibly die in such a beautiful river. Stanley and Livingstone and Speake and Akeley and Burton and others, they're all out there somewhere. I know these men; for more than a year, Joe and I brought them to life in the soft shade of a narrow river in western New York, and standing here now looking west I could sense them not far away, and Joe with them, talking about the changes, talking about the rain. I looked about the structures and vehicles and people all not far from me, and I wondered if it was possible that I knew more about this river than any of these people. Joe was right; it wasn't so scary once I was here. There are stores and I can go in and fumble my French or Swahili and purchase food, or barter. It felt like I fell into a map on one of the tables at the library, like in some book by Chesterton, and the only way out of here and back to my life is by moving forward.

I needed a canoe or a raft, supplies, that's all, and I could follow the bends and turns I knew so well from the maps we studied beneath lamps in a library six thousand miles away. I could follow Joe as Stanley had followed Livingstone, and as I was warned would happen in the mystical grip of the Congo, reason evaporated into the green hills of what was then called Zaire.

Surely, this earth of ours was patient with Joe, I thought, despite its obvious unpredictable temperament. But this was the wilds of Zaire, present day Democratic Republic of Congo, noted by all authorities as one of the most dangerous regions in the world. Still, in the 1980s when this narrative plays out, such danger, when there was any, was more predictable and, therefore, avoidable.

I looked west, and half of me felt lighter, energetic, brought to life by some African adrenaline Joe had warned me about, and whose source lay out before me. I would gather the supplies; of course, nothing else made sense. I was as ready as Joe was, obviously. We trained together; we learned the astronomy and dangers, the medical concerns, the river's turn, the villagers' anger and ease, together. "Our trip." Joe was at least over-enthusiastic, and more often than not certain of his success. That might have been his demise. I could do this; of course I could. I had something Joe never entertained—doubt. His confidence brought him seemingly without incident from Buffalo to Belem by bike, to the Congo, to the Amazon, and his insistence that I ride on my own from Virginia to Coos Bay, Oregon, which at the time was welcome support from an "adult" to this fifteen-year-old, in retrospect his support was tinged with carelessness. But in the years since our immersion into Joe's journey, when we waded through documents lost in the Congo in western New York, I've tempered his unabashed energy with my own dollop of caution. Standing waist deep in the river, surrounded by fisherman and industry, commerce and some sort of ancient presence, the spirit of place insisted I was ready to conquer the Congo on my own.

Standing now alone on the river, those placemat maps and the real maps the State Department sent, and the books about this place, the stories he told of this place, once nearly fantastical, are all real. After more than enough time of secondary tales, I finally stood in the midst of the primary source knowing somewhere not far away were answers. I was convinced my self-garnered expertise on the subject would be enough. "Where did you get your information?" I had been trained to be able to answer. Hell, yeah.

"Here," I thought. "Right here."

I stood waist deep and my mind ricocheted between the innocence of western New York and the visceral reality of the Congo River. How simple it was, back then, back there. How quixotic. How dreadfully and beautifully simple when I still thought this world of ours was all-welcoming and navigable. Most freshmen in college are most influenced by roommates and floormates and classmates—other freshmen, new friends who together learn to push away from their parents. I was just nineteen and instead of palling around with the ninety guys on my dorm floor to help me navigate into adulthood, who should take the helm but a world-class adventurer. He didn't steer me wrong, either. It's supposed to be like this, life, sometimes moving beyond our routines to something more challenging.

Before he left, Joe said, "Maybe I am trying to find myself." Indeed. Perhaps the possibility of dying in Africa didn't scare Joe half as much as ending up missing in civilization, drowned in the dysentery of ordinary life; a fear and burden I carried with me from then to this day. I understood Joe's passion. I've been staring at nineteen-year-olds for more than thirty-five years and that internal motivation, that spark for something "other than," is absent. Today they mostly look down, rarely noticing even each other, let alone adventure.

I looked out across this landscape suddenly awash with absolute presence; I stood in that rarest of states of no thoughts of what was or what's next. It was just me and the river, and I felt totally safe.

The Congo moves through the trees like blood in the veins, and the hills pulsate, the sky covers it all in a blue light, and the river runs brown but not dirty. It all blends into some organic aspect of existence, womb-like, and it feels comfortable, as if nothing could possibly hurt anyone here. The reality of Joe's disappearance suddenly didn't bother me here, nor his incomplete journey, if that is even possible, nor my own. Later, others asked why I went since I knew I wouldn't find out anything new. But that's not true. In fact, I discovered something very ancient, as primeval as Africa herself, and it is probably what called Conrad, and Stanley, Livingstone, and Kohn. Like the first explorers a millennium earlier, I carried the brand new to me, yet ancient concept that despite our hopes and expectations, all journeys are, in fact, incomplete.

I fixed on our final moments in the stairwell when he told me to get maps of the Amazon. I recalled stories of the villagers not far from here where he lived; I pictured a painting one villager made of the river. For years I pictured here, this spot, the sensation of dark water running around my ankles, the coarse sand under my shoes.

I remembered cutting up sun-dried fish not far from campus, laughing about the previous night's antics and conversations at Antonio's. Now on the Congo I felt somewhat at peace because of so much study and anticipation, but I knew beyond thought I didn't belong here either.

Still, I stared upriver and knew for certain not far away were answers . The water curled around my waist, and with absolute clarity, I thought, *this is not the Congo.*

This is the Allegheny.
This is 1981.
I'm not looking for Joe at all. It's me that's lost in the Congo.

Campus should be right there, across the hill, and students should be staggering toward breakfast smelling of beer. A student should be walking by and giving us a wave, laughing at our splashing about in the shallow water. At any moment, Joe will emerge and suggest we dry some fish in the sun to eat later. I should be younger, and the river should be cooler, flowing southwest toward Pennsylvania. I should be more awake, more alive. I should be sitting at a table for six at Antonio's, surrounded by friends laughing, Joe just to my left, steering the conversation.

The skies turned grey, and it started to rain. My face was wet, and I waded back to shore thinking about the overshadowed distances. We bury our dead. We have a wake, a funeral, and we bury them. When time passes, we remember them. Sometimes we visit their grave, and sometimes we bring flowers. But what do we do when someone disappears? Part of us never moves beyond the last moments with that person. There are no last rites. We simply wait.

Planning this impossible trip to the remote regions of the Congo was the first thing I ever did as an adult. Before I discussed any career with counselors or parents, before I thought about living on my own or where I'd like to find a job, before I had ever owned a car or had a steady girlfriend, I immersed myself in planning a trip to the remote river region of central Africa, with all the cultural, linguistic, medicinal, and emotional investments involved. That's how I started this life journey I'm on, and since then it has been easy to feel unchallenged; lost even.

I was quiet for a very long time. There are moments that never leave you; ones which to suggest you "remember" them is to do them a grave injustice, because it isn't memory, it is permanently part of your DNA so that simply to recall the moment is to feel the cool water around your waist, the current tugging at your shoes. To remember is to feel a coldness in your spine because you know you have to keep going. This was one of those moments, and I looked upriver with an absolute conviction that I would gather whatever supplies I could to continue this trip.

I reviewed the rules one must follow as I learned them in the quiet warmth of the college library one winter years earlier, partly out of habit, partly out of a review, a quick recap. First, people must travel lightly, remain in the middle, away from the dangerous shore and its overhanging branches. They look for skid marks made by crocs moving in and out of water. They avoid the wet, fresh skid. They don't reach below the surface, don't reach into the trees, don't wander too far from shore, don't stay too close. They can't sleep near the water nor too far from shore. Everyone avoids meat for possible contamination, fish for the same reason. Foreigners let villagers talk first to isolate and identify their language. They don't let anyone see a gun or large knife but don't travel without one. The Congo remains one of the most unpredictable areas on the planet where even nature's laws are often irrelevant.

I could start this right now, I thought.

God, what a time it was. What unbridled energy we had.

Stanley split the trip into two segments. Livingstone entered the region from the east, Conrad from the west. Joe started in the southeast and ended somewhere west of here. They all wrote of villages that moved because of drought or rain or war. They all wrote with confidence and assurance to whoever read the journals or letters or wires that the trip proceeded well and that great goals would be reached. Standing in the shallows of this great reach west I wondered how anyone could *not* travel on this river?

On the way to Kolwezi, my driver said, "Clearly your friend perished quite some time ago." I could not possibly explain to him something I would only come to realize myself when I arrived at the river. This wasn't about Joe.

My mind sailed between two worlds: one of innocence on desktops in western New York where these villages and river lines leaped off the page begging me to explore and discover their origins and mysteries, and another of the red clay and brown dust on the languid green hills of Zaire beneath my feet. My lack of understanding concerning this river forced me to search the most dangerous and remote region of AIDS-ridden, rebel-occupied, animal-dominated Zaire for someone I already knew was dead. Africa has always been a wild mare, and explorer after explorer followed each other into the corral, saying, "Let me have a go at her." Joe stood in line, and when his turn came, he had already studied what the others had done, where they had failed, succeeded, or, more importantly, what they had not yet attempted. Better to approach this bucking territory anew, see it from a different perspective.

The rain soaked my shirt and I stood staring west for ten minutes, silent, deciding. I remembered Stanley's diaries. On February 3rd, 1875, he wrote, "Livingstone called floating down the Lualaba a foolhardy feat. So it is, and were I to do it again, I would not attempt it without two hundred guns. We have no interpreter, and we cannot make ourselves understood. Still, I persist in continuing the journey." And he did so again in 1881, one hundred years before Joe pushed off near Lubumbashi, and at some point, he rowed by or stood exactly where I stood, the primary source. I wondered how far west I might find signs of Joe's passing. How far back would I have to continue traveling to find him again?

It did not escape me while standing in the river that I was the same age then as Joe was when he disappeared. It turns out after all of that planning and excitement, we were both lost.

Still, today, I remember when I was just nineteen years old that we planned an adventure of such enormous ambition, it is inconceivable anymore that that young man was me. We didn't know, of course, that the year we spent laughing, telling stories, deeply immersed in all-things Congo, surrounded by new friends in the library and at the restaurant, would turn out to be the adventure.

*The wain upon the northern steep
Descends and lifts away.
Oh, I will sit me down and weep
For bones in Africa*

—A. E. Housman

Epilogue

It's been a journey.

Kolwezi has changed since I was there. Bukavu resembles a large refugee camp. The small village of Moma simply doesn't exist anymore.

At some point, President Mobutu wanted government control of the mineral-rich region near Kolwezi. In 1992, a conference of ministers convened and appointed a new Prime Minister, Etienne Tshisekedi, to rule with Mobutu. But Tshisekedi refused to recognize Mobutu's authority after the President tried to fire him. The country suddenly had two separate governments. Security forces led by Mobutu's brother-in-law supported the president. Mobutu paid the army in Zaire notes, but they were quickly declared worthless, so the army looted the countryside. They pillaged stores, houses, and factories. Tshisekedi demanded democratic reform but received no cooperation from opposition parties. The army in response brutally attacked, mutilated, raped, and killed politicians, officials, priests, nuns, and journalists. This led to ethnic violence, and most of this occurred in the Shaba Province, not far from Kolwezi.

Reports emerged of soldiers cutting off people's arms, roasting and eating them, then tossing the still-moaning bodies onto the fire. Other soldiers further north hacked people open with machetes and spilled their organs on the ground next to them for animals to devour.

These stories are typical, occurring less than ten years after my travels. Animal and human carcasses could be seen floating down the river past Kolwezi. People were burned alive in their homes. In Moma, the Lendu burned fifteen huts and slaughtered all the inhabitants.

The DRC conflict has claimed an estimated four or five million lives, though most of them through hunger and disease. The New York based Rescue Committee reported that the Congo Rebellions are the deadliest conflicts since World War Two. The portrait Conrad painted of a daunting, dark world appears to be a reality in the Congo.

The Africa Joe talked about with tender language and sympathetic detail doesn't exist anymore. When I look at the maps, the mystery and energy they once provided are gone. Today, the south-central Congo River region is considered one of the most dangerous places on the planet for the wars and factions trying to gain control over the cobalt mines which contain over seventy percent of the world's supply that is needed for the batteries in Smartphones and electric vehicles.

I stood there once, waist deep, looking west.

So many players in this story are gone, and those that do remember don't care so much anymore. Little attention is paid to "almost" and "nearly." Adventures don't work that way. Maybe that's why it has taken so long to write this book: I'm still trying to finish that fucking trip.

Several months ago I went to the library to find an audio-book to bring on a drive to Florida. I chose, for no particular reason other than I had read the book when I was young, Beryl Markam's *West with the Night*. The choice had nothing to do with Joe or Africa or the trip. I chose it because all the other audiobooks available were fiction and I wanted something true.

I went to Florida, however, without listening to it. On the way home I turned it on, and it starts with Markam explaining that she has no idea how to start this book, that it can start in so many different ways. I listen for a while but eventually my mind returns to this manuscript, which at that point was neatly tucked away under a stack of books at my desk since I simply had no idea how to start it, and it had been quite some time since I revisited the narrative. I listened to the book the rest of the way home, and that night pulled out the manuscript for *Curious Men* and reread the first page. My enthusiasm waned when I realized I'd have to actually make it work as well as Markam had in her brilliant prose.

So like any writer worth their salt would do at that moment, I chose procrastination, and instead I rifled through my messages which had arrived while I was away. One in particular from someone unknown had been sent earlier that day.

It was from Kim Kohn Lindfors, Joe's young sister he drove to kindergarten before leaving for Africa that last time. She wrote that evening to tell me her father had died the previous September, in 2024. On this very evening spread out on my desk was this manuscript about her brother, which I looked at for the first time in a long time, and she asked if I had ever finished the book about him she knew I was writing. I told her that I was sorry I hadn't finished it in time for her dad to read it, but it was on my desk, and she said she had read him a chapter from it that had been published in a journal. Everything felt too real again to turn away.

Forty years collapsed into some immediacy I can't explain, as if only one night had passed since Joe boarded the taxi at the college, and I was still shaking away the sleep. She recalled for me the few memories she had of him, including him driving her to school. She said she remembered the coat that he wears in the picture of him and me with a college friend, Annemarie Wess (Franczyk).

Some stories perhaps shouldn't be told, or maybe they can't be told well enough to bother starting them at all. This might be one of those stories. But something in this narrative of my life back then kept scratching at my consciousness. It took a long time for me to understand what it wanted to say. Maybe because I've been staring at nineteen-year-olds for thirty-five years I now have a better perspective.

It is difficult to ever know how to find that thin line between a plan failing and the plan succeeding. That the difference between never seen again and governments naming waterways after him can be separated by just split seconds on the shoreline of a tributary, a few pills short of getting better, the false sense he can't take one more day to rest. Who knows which person deemed by society to be a failure—or worse, never even recognized as existing at all—was a hair away from inspiring a generation?

And now more than forty years after the adventure when we spent those days and nights at Antonio's and the library lost in the Congo, one thing is certain: All journeys are incomplete.

Postscript: the Congo River was conquered solo by Phil Harwood in 2008, twenty-seven years after Joe wrote his last letters from Kolwezi. Phil's account is recalled in his memoir, *Canoeing the Congo*.

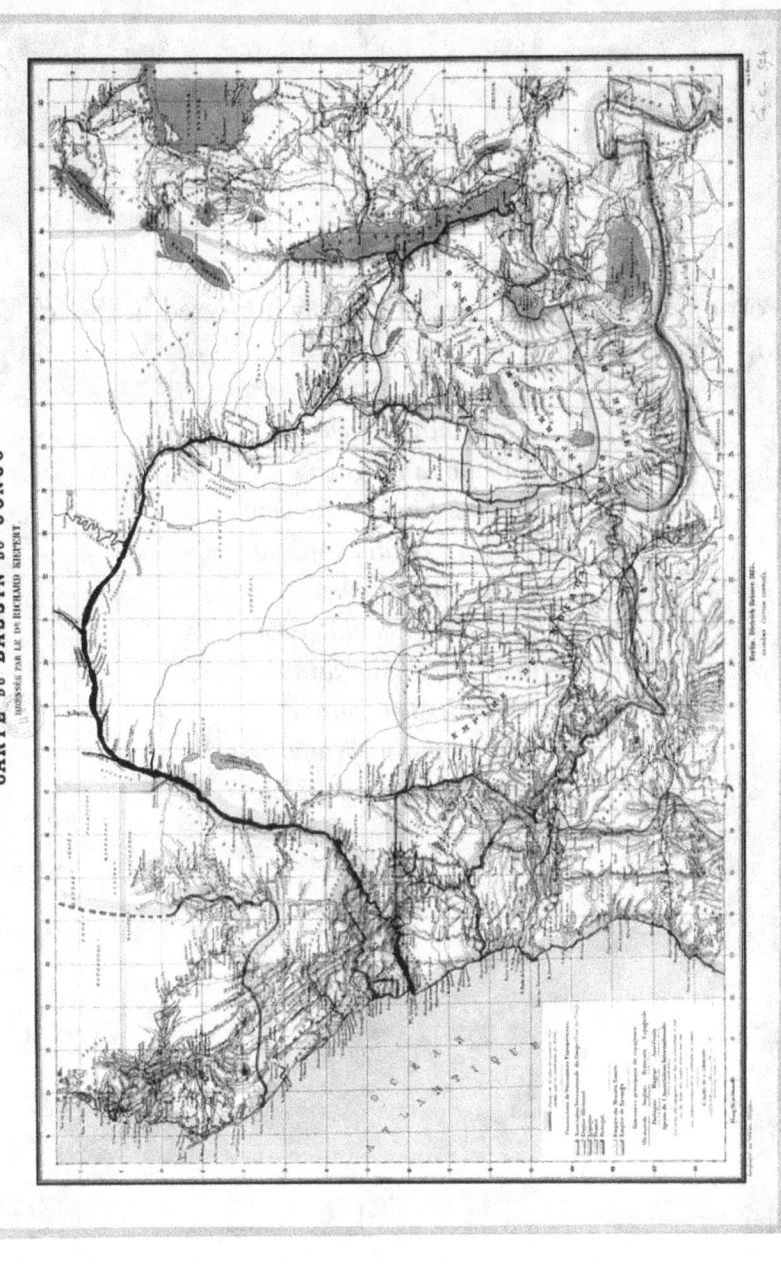

Portions of this work have previously appeared in the following publications:

Ilanot Review
Palooka Magazine
Alabama Literary Review
Foreign Literary Journal
Matador Review
The Buffalo Evening News
Borderline Crazy (All Nations Press)
Wanderlust Journal
A View from this Wilderness
The Buffalo Evening News

About the Author

Bob Kunzinger is the author of a dozen non-fiction works, including *The Iron Scar: A Father and Son in Siberia*, and *Out of Nowhere: Scenes from St. Petersburg*. His work has appeared in many publications. He lives along the Rappahannock River in Virginia.

About the Author

Bob Kanzuger is the author of 7 other nonfiction works, including *The Iraq Soldier Institute*, *Grown up Nation*, and *Out of Nowhere: Scenes from the Peacetime*. His work has appeared in many public sheets. He lives along the Rappahannock River in Virginia.